THE LAST GENERATION, THE RAPTURE, AND THE WRATH

T0078210

THE LAST GENERATION, THE RAPTURE, AND THE WRATH

SUNDAY OLUSOLA FALUYI

iUniverse LLC
Bloomington

THE LAST GENERATION, THE RAPTURE, AND THE WRATH

iUniverse books may be ordered through booksellers or by contacting:

iUniverse LLC
1663 Liberty Drive
Bloomington, IN 47403
www.iuniverse.com
1-800-Authors (1-800-288-4677)

ISBN: 978-1-4759-7587-1 (sc)
ISBN: 978-1-4759-7588-8 (e)

Printed in the United States of America

iUniverse rev. date: 11/04/2013

Table of Contents

Dedication vii
Acknowledgements ix
Introduction xi

Chapter One
  Order of End-Time Events According to Jesus Christ 1
Chapter Two
  Sign of the Last Generation 12
Chapter Three
  The Sign of the Six Days 24
Chapter Four
  Sign of the Year of Jubilee 27
Chapter Five
  First, Second, and Third Seals 45
Chapter Six
  Fourth Seal Part 1: Middle East War
    (September 2015-2022) 57
Chapter Seven
  Fourth Seal Part II: World War III
    (September 2015-2022) 70
Chapter Eight
  The Little Horn, the Beast, and the False Prophet
    (September 2015-2022) 80
Chapter Nine
  Fifth Seal Part I: The Tribulation Period
    (September 2022-2029 A.D.) 95
Chapter Ten
  Fifth Seal Part II: Seven-Year Peace Treaty and
    the Great Tribulation (September 2022-2029 A.D.) 103
Chapter Eleven
  Sixth Seal: The Rapture and the Marriage Supper
    of the Lamb 118

Chapter Twelve
    Seventh Seal Part I: The Wrath of God............................126
Chapter Thirteen
    Seventh Seal Part 2: Fourth World War and
        the Greatest Earthquake (2029-2036 A.D.)..............136
Chapter Fourteen
    The Great Millennium: One-Thousand Years of Peace..... 158
Chapter Fifteen
    Who Is This Christ?..161
Chapter Sixteen
    Conclusion..167

Appendix
    Calculating the Days from Adam..................................171

Dedication

This book is dedicated to men and women chosen by God to overcome evil by the blood of the Lamb and by the word of their testimony; because they love not their lives unto death (Rev. 12:11).

Acknowledgements

To my Lord and Savior, Jesus Christ, who has called me out of darkness into his marvelous light and who has commissioned me to take the gospel to the nations. To my wife, Omolara, who has supported, encouraged, advised, and contributed immensely from the beginning to the end of this project. To Pastor Bamgbopa Gbolahan and the entire congregation of the Redeemed Christian Church of God: Praise Court Parish, Far Rockaway, New York, for their incessant prayers and support. To Brother Victor Ugochukwu, my co-worker in Christ's vineyard, whose professional touch led to invaluable suggestions and contributions. To Dr. Theophilus Olumese, whose prayers, critiques, contributions, and interest helped me immensely during the writing of this book. To Dr. Seun Arimoro, Reverend (Doctor) John Mubenwafor and Brother Abraham Ajewole, whose prayers, comments, and insights contributed in many ways to the successful conclusion of this project. To Marvin Rosenthal, the executive director of Zion's Hope (a faith mission), whose book, *The Pre-Wrath Rapture of the Church: A New Understanding of the Rapture, the Tribulation, and the Second Coming*, helped me during the research phase. To H. L. Nigro, founder of Strong Tower Publishing, whose work, *Before God's Wrath: The Bible's Answer to the Timing of the Rapture* provided new insights during the research phase and who is also the editor of this book.

Introduction

Nations are on the verge of civil war; the foundation for a cataclysmic nuclear war is gradually being laid; terrorism has become pandemic, and the war against it is raging from one end of the globe to the other. Internecine, ethno-religious wars are on the increase; and fear, joblessness, hopelessness, and helplessness have become an epidemic. Capitalism is on the decline and socialism is gradually replacing it as the new world order. The world is in complete disarray. It is racing madly toward Armageddon.

Bible students with eschatological insight know that this is the time of the end. The coming of the Lord Jesus is at hand. Unfortunately, like the biblical foolish virgins, many are not paying attention. They are not prepared. They have failed to realize that this generation will witness the things Jesus revealed to John in the apocalyptic book of Revelation.

The purpose of this book is to sound the alarm on God's holy hill, with the clear intent that this clarion call will stir up the church and cause her to purify and make herself ready for the coming of the Lord. Everyone who has this hope in Christ purifies himself just as Christ is pure (1 John 3:3). So that when Jesus descends from heaven with the voice of the archangel and the trump of God (1 Thess. 4:17), he will receive to himself a glorious church without spot, wrinkle, or blemish (Eph. 5:27).

Be blessed!

Chapter One

Order of End-Time Events According to Jesus Christ

Jesus in his wisdom gave us the order of end-time events in Matthew's gospel as well as in the book of Revelation chapters five through seven. Though end-time Bible scholars agree that the eschatological events about which Jesus prophesied will eventually come to pass, the order of their fulfillment is a thorny and divisive issue. My take is that the words of Jesus must be taken literally.

Jesus gave the order of end-time events not once, but twice. Whenever Jesus opens his mouth to speak, what comes out is truth—absolute truth. Jesus' sayings are not subject to theological debate. What he says will come first will come first, and what he says will come last will come last. It is wise for the saints of the living God to take this order of events seriously. According to the book of Revelation, the order of events is sealed and unchangeable. It shall be according to the Word of God.

These events were predicted by Jesus two thousand years ago. Now they are coming to pass in our generation in the exact order he prophesied. We expect no less from someone who is the beginning and the end, the one who declared without ambiguity or equivocation:

> "Heaven and earth will pass away, but my words
> will by no means pass away." (Matt. 24:35)

On the Mount of Olives during the last week of his earthly ministry, Jesus told his disciples about the concatenation or series of events that would characterize the end time. This discourse was recorded in the synoptic gospels of Matthew, Mark, and Luke. In this chapter, I will juxtapose the twenty-fourth chapter of the gospel according to Mathew with chapters five through seven of Revelation. This will reveal an amazing truth. In Matthew 24 and Revelation chapters 5-7, the order of end-time events is exactly the same. In Revelation, Jesus simply added more detail. My reason for comparing them is twofold: to show the similarities between the prophecies in the two books with the hope that it will make the book of Revelation easier to understand and to encourage us to take the order of eschatological events very seriously.

Matthew 24	Revelation 5, 6, and 7
Introduction	**Introduction**
Then Jesus went out and departed from the temple, and his disciples came up to show him the buildings of the temple. And Jesus said to them, "Do you not see all these things? Assuredly, I say to you, not one stone shall be left here upon another, that shall not be thrown down."	And I saw in the right hand of him who sat on the throne a scroll written inside and on the back, sealed with seven seals. Then I saw a strong angel proclaiming with a loud voice, "Who is worthy to open the scroll and to loose its seals?" And no one in heaven or on the earth or under the earth was able to open the scroll, or to look at it. (Rev. 5:1-3)
Now as he sat on the Mount of Olives, the disciples came to him privately, saying, "Tell us, when will these things be? And what will be the sign of your coming, and of the end of the age?" (Matt. 24:1-3)	And I looked, and behold, in the midst of the throne and of the four living creatures, and in the midst of the elders, stood a Lamb as though it had been slain, having seven horns and seven eyes, which are the seven Spirits of God sent out into all the earth. Then he came and took the scroll out of the right hand of him who sat on the throne. (Rev. 5:6-7)
Note: The prophecy given in verse two was fulfilled in 70 A.D. when the temple in Jerusalem was destroyed by Roman soldiers under the command of Titus. The destruction of the temple	

was total. No stone was left standing. Jesus Christ was 100 percent accurate	
First Event: False Christ/False Peace	**First Seal: False Christ/ False Peace**
And Jesus answered and said to them: "Take heed that no one deceives you. For many will come in my name, saying, '*I am the Christ,*' and will deceive many." (Matt 24: 4-5, emphasis mine)	Now I saw when the Lamb opened one of the seals; and I heard one of the four living creatures saying with a voice like thunder, "Come and see." And I looked, and behold, a white horse. *He who sat on it had a bow; and a crown was given to him,* and he went out conquering and to conquer. (Rev. 6:1-2, emphasis mine)
Second Event: Peace Is Taken from the Earth	**Second Seal: Peace Is Taken from the Earth**
"*And you will hear of wars and rumors of wars.* See that you are not troubled; for all these things must come to pass, but the end is not yet." (Matt. 24:6, emphasis mine)	When he opened the second seal, I heard the second living creature saying, "Come and see." Another horse, fiery red, went out. *And it was granted to the one who sat on it to take peace from the earth, and that people should kill one another;* and there was given to him a great sword. (Rev. 6: 3-4, emphasis mine)
Third Event: Global Economic Crisis	**Third Seal: Global Economic Crisis**
"And there will be *famines,* pestilences, and earthquakes in various places." (Matt. 24:7, emphasis mine)	When he opened the third seal, I heard the third living creature say, "Come and see." So I looked, and behold, a black horse, and he who sat on it had a pair of scales in his hand. *And I heard a voice in the midst of the four living creatures saying, "A quart of wheat for a denarius, and three quarts of barley for a denarius*

	[global scarcity]; and do not harm the oil and the wine." (Rev. 6:5-6, emphasis mine)
Fourth Event: War "*For nation will rise against nation, and kingdom against kingdom . . . .* All these are the beginning of sorrows." (Matt. 24:7,8, emphasis mine)	**Fourth Seal: War** When he opened the fourth seal, I heard the voice of the fourth living creature saying, "Come and see." So I looked, and behold, a pale horse. And the name of him who sat on it was Death, and Hades followed with him. *And power was given to them over a fourth of the earth, to kill with sword, with hunger, with death, and by the beasts of the earth.* (Rev. 6:7-8, emphasis mine)
Fifth Event 5a: Great Persecution of the Followers of Christ "*Then they will deliver you up to tribulation and kill you,* and you will be hated by all nations for my name's sake . . . And this gospel of the kingdom will be preached in all the world as a witness to all the nations, and then the end will come." (Matt 24: 9-14, emphasis mine)	**Fifth Seal 5a: Great Persecution of the Followers of Christ** When he opened the fifth seal, *I saw under the altar the souls of those who had been slain for the word of God and for the testimony which they held.* And they cried with a loud voice, saying, "How long, O Lord, holy and true, until you judge and avenge our blood on those who dwell on the earth?" (Rev. 6:9-10, emphasis mine)
5b. The Coming Great Jewish Holocaust "Therefore when you see the 'abomination of desolation,' spoken of by Daniel the prophet, standing in the holy place" (whoever reads, let him understand), "then let those who are in Judea	**5b. The Coming Great Jewish Holocaust** Then a white robe was given to each of them; and it was said to them that they should rest a little while longer, *until both the number of their fellow servants and their brethren, who would be killed*

flee to the mountains . . . *For then there will be great tribulation, such as has not been since the beginning of the world until this time, no, nor ever shall be.* And unless those days were shortened, no flesh would be saved; but for the elect's sake those days will be shortened. (Matt. 24:15-22, emphasis mine)	*as they were, was completed.* (Rev. 6:11, emphasis mine)
Sixth Event: The Rapture	**Sixth Seal: The Rapture**
"Immediately after the tribulation of those *days the sun will be darkened, and the moon will not give its light; the stars will fall from heaven, and the powers of the heavens will be shaken. Then the sign of the Son of Man will appear in heaven,* and then all the tribes of the earth will mourn, and they will see the Son of Man coming on the clouds of heaven with power and great glory. And he will send his angels with a great sound of a trumpet, *and they will gather together his elect from the four winds, from one end of heaven to the other.*" (Matt. 24: 29-31, emphasis mine)	I looked when he opened the sixth seal, and behold, there was a great earthquake; *and the sun became black as sackcloth of hair, and the moon became like blood. And the stars of heaven fell to the earth,* as a fig tree drops its late figs when it is shaken by a mighty wind. Then the sky receded as a scroll when it is rolled up, and every mountain and island was moved out of its place . . . (Rev. 6:12-17, emphasis mine) *After these things I looked, and behold, a great multitude which no one could number, of all nations, tribes, peoples, and tongues, standing before the throne and before the Lamb, clothed with white robes, . . . These are the ones who come out of the great tribulation, and washed their robes and made them white in the blood of the Lamb . . .* And God will wipe away every tear from their eyes." (Rev. 7: 9-17, emphasis mine)

	Seventh Seal
	[Author paraphrase:] During this time, the wrath of God is revealed. The seven trumpets of judgment bring down the fierce anger of God upon the inhabitants of the earth. Simultaneously, the wrath of God in the bowls ushers in the worst crisis in human history. These judgments will be discussed in detail in the latter part of this book.

Close scrutiny of the list of major end-time events highlighted in Matthew 24 and the book of Revelation makes one scriptural fact unequivocally clear—the saints of God will go through tribulation (the fifth seal) but will escape the wrath of God (the seventh seal). It is unfortunate to note that, through much biblical literature, a clear distinction has not been made between these two end-time events. The result is confusion among many Christians. I want to declare without ambiguity or equivocation that tribulation should not and must not be confused with the wrath of God.

When the righteous, innocent, honest and just individuals are wrongly punished, unfairly attacked and killed for doing the right thing and/or for their testimony of the Lord Jesus Christ, it is tribulation.

There cannot be tribulation or persecution for wicked people. When criminals suffer for their wrongdoing, it is not tribulation but punishment. Hence, there cannot be tribulation after rapture. The wicked, the disobedient, the foolish and the unbelieving men and women that are left behind after rapture are going to suffer for rejecting Jesus Christ. It is this divine punishment that is called the wrath of God.

One way to make a distinction between tribulation and the wrath of God is to look for the source of the trouble, crisis or punishment. When the trouble is from the devil, we call it tribulation. When it is from God, we call it the wrath of God. This is important because many times tribulation is directed toward the saints. Hence, Jesus Christ comforted the disciples with this message: "These things I have spoken to you, that in me you may have peace. In the world you will have tribulation; but be of good cheer, I have overcome the world" (John 16:33). Conversely, the wrath of God is always directed towards the disobedient. For instance, Jonah (Jonah 1:4, 17) and David (1 Chron. 21:7-15) experienced the wrath of God because of disobedience. To reject Jesus Christ is disobedience; therefore, the end-time wrath of God is directed towards a Christ-rejecting world.

Tribulation of the Saints

Tribulation can be referred to as the murderous intent, wrath, unrighteous anger or persecution of the people of the living God by Satan, the devil. For instance, the oppression of the children of Israel in Egypt by Pharaoh was a form of tribulation (Ex. 1:15-16). There was a clandestine and calculated attempt to destroy the seed of Abraham but as usual, Satan failed woefully. Another example of tribulation is the experience of the three Hebrew boys in Babylon when they refused to worship the idol set up by King Nebuchadnezzar. These three men were thrown into a blazing furnace. But the living and faithful God stepped in to deliver his own. (Dan. 3:24-25)

The anger of the devil against the people of God is what tribulation is all about. Although these three Hebrew boys went through tribulation, the presence of Jesus, the fourth man in the fiery furnace, gave them victory. In the same vein, as Christians, we also will have to endure tribulation that will test our faith as we press towards the mark for the prize of the high calling of God in Christ Jesus. Like the Hebrew children, we have this blessed assurance: Victory is certain in Jesus' name. Remember Daniel who was thrown into the lion's den for praying to God, but was miraculously delivered.

The Church of Christ Was Born in Tribulation

Scripture is replete with accounts of persecution of men and women of God and the tribulation they endured. On the day of Pentecost, in 33 A.D., the church of the living God was born. She came into manifestation with the power and glory of the Holy Spirit. On that day, Peter stood up and preached a power-packed message to his audience. The result? Three thousand people accepted Christ. But afterwards, Satan stirred up trouble against the newly founded church, and disciples such as Stephen, the first Christian martyr, and James, the brother of John, lost their lives.

The Church of Christ Grew Up in Tribulation

In the first century A.D., especially during the reign of Emperor Nero, many Christians were severely tortured, jailed, and killed for their witnesses to the resurrection of Jesus Christ. Yet, the church continued to grow. That is why Tertullian, a second-century theologian, declared that "the blood of the martyrs is the seed of the church." At the end of the third and the beginning of fourth centuries A.D., the persecution of Christians within the Roman Empire was so fierce that church worship was banned and Christian clergies were imprisoned. The persecution intensified until Christians living within the empire were commanded to sacrifice to the gods or face immediate execution. Over twenty thousand Christians were thought to have died during Diocletian's reign. Yet, the church grew until she dominated the empire.

Twentieth Century: The Century of Tribulation of the Saints

The tribulation that began in early days of the church has continued throughout history. In fact, the twentieth century has been called "the century of the tribulation of the saints."[1]Let's look at a few examples.

The Young Turks government of the collapsing Ottoman Empire in 1915 persecuted Christian populations in Anatolia. This persecution, resulting from the wars between Muslim and Christian populations at Syria and Mesopotamia, resulted in an estimated 2.1 million deaths, divided between roughly 1.2 million Armenian Christians, 0.6 million Syriac/Assyrian Christians, and 0.3 million Greek Orthodox Christians. A number of Georgians were also killed.

After the Revolution of 1917, the Bolsheviks undertook a massive program to remove the influence of the Russian Orthodox Church from the government and Russian society and create an atheist state. Tens of thousands of churches were destroyed or converted to other uses. Many members of the clergy were imprisoned for "anti-government" activities. An extensive education and propaganda campaign was undertaken to convince people, especially children and youth, to abandon their religious beliefs. This persecution resulted in the martyrdom of millions of Orthodox followers in the twentieth century by the Soviet Union, whether intentional or not.

In the twentieth century, there are thousands of documented cases of persecution by Christians in Spain, Poland, Iran, Sudan, India, Pakistan, Kosovo and Indonesia. For instance in China, the communist government of the People's Republic of China tries to maintain tight control over all religions; so the only legal Christian churches (Three-Self Patriotic Movement and

---

[1]   http://en.wikipedia.org/wiki/Persecution_of_Christians (last accessed June 21, 2012)

Chinese Patriotic Catholic Association) are those under the control of the Communist Party of China. Churches not controlled by the government are shut down and their members imprisoned.

Tribulation Is Ongoing

In other parts of the world, even in countries where you would least expect it, tribulation is on the increase. For instance, at the beginning of 2010, in East Texas, churches were burned in what authorities referred to as cases of arson. Moreover, documented cases of persecution against Christians including burning and destruction of churches are increasing in Nigeria, Egypt, Syria, Sudan, Iran and Afghanistan.

Great Tribulation Cometh

The last century witnessed the severe persecution of Christians on a large scale. However, we need to watch and pray because another *great* tribulation is coming. This is going to be evidenced within the next two decades. This great tribulation is the final attempt by Satan to annihilate the Jews and the followers of Christ. It is going to be the physical manifestation of a spiritual war in which Satan, the adversary and accuser of the children of God, will be defeated. The great tribulation will be an intense period in which the bride of Christ will be purged, prepared, cleansed, and made ready for the bridegroom. Though this period will be characterized by wickedness of mind-numbing proportions, it will also be a period of the greatest demonstration of the awesome power, glory, and faithfulness of God in the lives of those who trust in Him. The outpouring of the Holy Spirit during this period will be unparalleled in the history of the church. Signs and wonders will be common in the church of Christ. This fire of tribulation will separate the wheat from the tares as the Lord of Harvest prepares to establish his kingdom.

I perceive four waves of tribulation. The first wave will come with an attempt to establish a form of world religion in the name of peace. This powerful ecumenical movement backed by very powerful political activists in many countries will not tolerate dissenting views from some Christian denominations. Many bold Christians will be persecuted for their faith. This will lead to a schism and falling away by many from the faith. Those who depart from the faith will persecute those who are standing in it.

The second wave will come in the form of a World War III, while the third wave will be ushered in with an attempt to use microchips implanted in humans as a means of payment. The last and the final wave, known as the great tribulation, will come with an attempt to completely annihilate the state of Israel. Each of these waves will be addressed later in this book.

Chapter Two

Sign of the Last Generation

Many generations had expected Jesus Christ to come during their lifetimes. Even Paul, an apostle of Jesus Christ, expected the second coming of Jesus to occur in his day.

This is a good example of how to live as believers in Christ Jesus. We must live with the expectation that the Lord is coming soon. To be wise is to live our lives as if today is the last day. To be wise is to be ready to meet the Lord whenever the trumpet sounds. Therefore, today is the day of salvation; tomorrow may be too late.

Paul died about two thousand years ago without witnessing the coming of the Lord. After him, generations of Christians have lived with the same expectation that Christ will come in their lifetimes. While the Lord has not come, the signs of his soon appearing are all around us. In this chapter, I will do an exposition on four landmark prophecies that have been fulfilled.

The Parable of the Fig Tree

Let us begin exegesis (or exposition) on the fulfilled prophecies from the parable of the fig tree in Matthew 24. This parable identifies the generation that will witness the coming of our Lord.

> "Now learn this parable from the fig tree: When its branch has already become tender and puts forth leaves, you know that summer is near. So you

also, when you see all these things, know that it is near—at the doors! Assuredly, I say to you, *this generation will by no means pass away till all these things take place.* Heaven and earth will pass away, but my words will by no means pass away." (Matt. 24:32-35, emphasis mine)

In Scripture, the fig tree is symbolic of the nation of Israel. Three great prophets—Jeremiah, Hosea, and Joel—all referred to Israel as God's fig tree. For instance, Jeremiah divided the children of Israel into two camps—the good figs and the bad figs (Jer. 24:3-5, 8). The prophet Hosea clearly heard God liken the nation of Israel to a fig tree as well (Hosea 9:10). In his lamentation regarding the end-time invasion of the nation of Israel, Joel also referred to Israel as God's fig tree. (Joel 1:7)

By paying attention to biblical prophets, we know that the geographical space called Israel is God's fig tree. In the aforementioned parable, Jesus is admonishing us to pay attention to God's fig tree. A strategic lesson we need to learn is that God has given us means to understand His end-time agenda. He made Israel his prophetic clock. If we want to understand God's prophetic timetable for the end time, we need to look at Israel. In addition, Matthew 24:34 identifies a particular generation that will witness all of the end-time events from beginning to end. This generation is referred to as *the last generation.*

In this chapter, we are going to examine the last generation and its lifespan. I believe that we are the last generation, and that we are rushing aggressively toward the end. I hope this book will help you to reflect on your priorities as a child of God and run the race that is set before you.

The Last Generation

The last generation began with a notable end-time event, the restoration of Israel as foretold by the prophets of old.

God's end-time clock has started ticking. The countdown to the end has begun.

First Event: The Restoration of Israel (1948-present)

In 70 A.D., Jerusalem was attacked and defeated by Roman soldiers led by General Titus. The temple in that ancient city was burned down. For more than 1800 years, the children of Israel were scattered throughout the nations of the world. The ancient Hebrew language almost disappeared from the earth. Many Jews were oppressed, suppressed, and victimized in foreign lands. Though they made supplication to God daily for restoration because of his covenant with their father Abraham, they remained second-class citizens around the world. They were scorned, taunted, persecuted, and marginalized. It seemed as if God had forgotten his own people.

This was the origin of a doctrine called "replacement theology." This is the view that God has replaced the Jews with the church, that the church is the New Jerusalem, and that the promised restoration of Israel actually refers to the establishment of the kingdom of God. I could not disagree more. The Word of God cannot be used to negate God's covenant with Abraham.

According to the apostle Paul, in spite of the redemption of believers in Christ Jesus, the Jews will be saved. (Rom. 11:1, 11, 23-24)

The prophet Amos gave a very clear and concise account of the restoration of Israel. (Amos 9:14-15)

In this prophecy, God promised to bring the Jews back to their land, never to be uprooted again. Not only has God brought Israel back to their land as promised, but he has also restored the ancient Hebrew language. This is a warning to nations planning to destroy Israel: *You will fail.*

Why? Because the Bible makes it clear that Israel will not be annihilated.

The prophet Ezekiel also prophesied about the restoration of Israel as well as God's intent for doing so (Eze. 36:22-24). Ezekiel's prophecy was like a panoramic view of Israel's future. According to the prophet, the desolation of the land of Israel would be long. And long it was—more than 1800 years. What a great God! There is no nation in the history of the human race that has been restored after being left desolate for so long.

In 1948, the living God brought the Jews from the four corners of the earth back to their own land. His Word concerning their restoration was fulfilled with prophetic precision. That was the beginning of the restoration of God's fig tree. *The last generation started on May 14, 1948.* On that day, the nation of Israel was born.

On May 15, 1948, a day after the declaration of the new Jewish state, Israel was attacked by five neighboring Arab states—Lebanon, Syria, Jordan, Egypt, and Iraq—in an attempt to make the nation a still-born child. It was an attempt by the evil one to nullify God's Word, but it failed woefully. The Jews did not win the Israeli-Arab war because of their military might or ingenuity. They won because God was faithful to fulfill his Word that they would not be uprooted from their land again.

In 1956, Egypt nationalized the Suez Canal Company and closed the strategic shipping lane to Israel. As a result, Israel went to war against Egypt and won. Again, June 5-10, 1967, the popular Six-Day War erupted in the Middle East. Egypt, Lebanon, Syria, and Jordan attempted to encircle Israel. Moreover, the Arab states of Iraq, Saudi Arabia, Sudan, Algeria, Tunisia, and Morocco joined forces with the aforementioned triumvirate of Islamic nations against Israel. In that short and swift battle, Israel emerged as the winner and captured eastern Jerusalem and the Temple Mount (where Solomon's Temple once stood) from Jordan. Israel also captured the strategic Golan Heights from Syria. That victory gave a new coloration to the Middle East power game. It strengthened Israel's northern flank and gave hope to the possibility of rebuilding the temple in the near future.

On October 6, 1973, the Yom Kippur War started. Israel was attacked suddenly and simultaneously by the Egyptian Army from the south and the Syrian Army from the north. Israel was overwhelmed. When it appeared that she was going to lose the battle, God intervened. The tide turned suddenly; and once again, Israel won. The conflict led to a near confrontation between two nuclear superpowers, the United States and the former Soviet Union, both of which initiated massive resupply efforts to their allies during the war. An imposed ceasefire eventually led to the cessation of hostilities.

In 1981, Israel preemptively destroyed Iraq's nuclear facility. In September 2007, Israel, through an air strike, destroyed a complex in the Syrian Desert that many believed to be a nuclear reactor. God has been faithful to his Word. Israel has fought and won several battles in the past fifty-two years. The next big war is coming soon. This will be discussed in detail under the fourth seal because it is going to trigger the World War III.

Second Event: The Revival of Roman Empire (1954-Present)

After the resurrection of the Jewish nation, another historic event took place: the power, the glory, and the spirit of the ancient Roman Empire were revived. According to Daniel, four empires would rule the world, but the last one would be a confederate of ten nations. Daniel gave that revelation while narrating the dream of King Nebuchadnezzar of Babylon:

> You, O king, are a king of kings . . . you are this head of gold. But after you shall arise another kingdom inferior to yours; then another, a third

16

kingdom of bronze, which shall rule over all the earth. And the fourth kingdom shall be as strong as iron, in as much as iron breaks in pieces and shatters everything; and like iron that crushes, that kingdom will break in pieces and crush all the others. Whereas you saw the feet and toes, partly of potter's clay and partly of iron, the kingdom shall be divided; yet the strength of the iron shall be in it, just as you saw the iron mixed with ceramic clay. And as the toes of the feet were partly of iron and partly of clay, so the kingdom shall be partly strong and partly fragile. As you saw iron mixed with ceramic clay, they will mingle with the seed of men; but they will not adhere to one another, just as iron does not mix with clay. And in the days of these kings the God of heaven will set up a kingdom which shall never be destroyed. (Dan. 2:36-44)

History tells us that the kingdoms in successive order are as follows:

1. Babylonian Empire (the head of gold)
2. Medo-Persian Empire (the chest and arms of silver)
3. Greek Empire (the belly and thighs of bronze)
4. Roman Empire (the legs of iron which extend to the feet and toes of combined clay and iron)

Let us pay attention to the fourth kingdom. The Roman Empire, which started as a republic, was fully established by 27 B.C. during the reign of Caesar Augustus. This empire grew until it was divided into the western and eastern empires, represented by the two legs of the huge image in Nebuchadnezzar's dream. Whereas the eastern part of the Roman Empire endured until the fifteenth century (when it was replaced by the Ottoman Empire), the western part of the empire fell in the fifth century.

However, Daniel predicted how the Roman Empire would ultimately end. In Nebuchadnezzar's dream, the two legs ended in ten toes, signifying that in the latter times, the

Roman Empire will be revived as a confederation of ten nations. Because the dissolution of the Roman Empire occurred centuries ago, this prophecy tells us that, sometime in the future, the empire will be revived to rule the whole world again. Since the feet and toes are made up of clay and iron, the coming Revived Roman Empire will be partly strong because it will consist of very influential nations and partly fragile because it will also consist of some weak nations.

Daniel also said: "In the days of these kings the God of heaven will set up a kingdom which shall never be destroyed." (Dan. 2:44) This implies that the coming of Christ to establish the kingdom of God will coincide with the time the Revived Roman Empire will be exercising political authority over the whole world. I believe this is going to happen within the lifespan of this current generation.

It is amazing to see the coming into being of the Revived Roman Empire right before our eyes. With the signing of the Treaty of Rome on March 25, 1957 by West Germany, Italy, France, Luxembourg, Netherlands, and Belgium, the European Economic Community (EEC) was born. What started as a proposition started to become a reality. In 1993, the European Union was formally established. In 2002, the euro, the common currency of the EEC, was launched. In 2009, the first president of the European Council was elected. As at the writing of this book, there are 27 member states from Europe that are being integrated together to form a stronger European Union.

The Western European Union (WEU) has ten member countries, six associate member countries, five observer countries, and seven associate partner countries. On June 14, 2001, Javier Solana, the former High Representative for Common Foreign and Security Policy of the European Union, stated that there was no foreseeable reason to change the status of the non-member countries. The ten member countries are fixed. These are the ten toes of the Book of Daniel and the ten horns of the Book of Revelation.

Member Countries: (Modified Brussels Treaty—1954)

1. Belgium
2. France
3. Germany
4. Greece
5. Italy
6. Luxembourg
7. The Netherlands
8. Portugal
9. Spain
10. The United Kingdom

These ten countries are members of both NATO and the European Union. They are the only nations with full voting rights. In 1995, Greece became the last nation to be admitted into full membership. Therefore, in 1999 when three members of NATO (Hungary, Poland, and the Czech Republic) joined the European Union, they were not admitted into full membership of the WEU.

These ten nations, in partnership with the United States of America, will take over the political and economic power of the whole world in the nearest future. For now, they represent the soul and backbone of the European Union. For instance, the current president of the European Commission is Jose Manuel Barroso from Portugal. He was elected to a five-year term in 2009. At that time, the four topmost contenders for the post of the president of Europe came from Belgium, The Netherlands, Luxembourg, and the United Kingdom. We can see that these ten nations will continue to dominate the political, economic, social, and military agenda of the European Union.

On November 19, 2009, the first president of Europe was elected. He is the Belgian Prime Minister, Herman Van Rompuy. History is being made in this generation—an empire that received a fatal blow in the fifth century is coming back to life to take control of the global political and socio-economic power of the world as predicted by Daniel more than twenty-five hundred years ago.

Third Event: Revolution in the Communication System (1957-Present)

When John penned the book of Revelation about nineteen hundred years ago, he described a situation that must have appeared impossible to the people of his time. In chapter eleven, he prophesied that God would raise two prophets in the last days. These two prophets will meet their demise in Jerusalem after the completion of their prophetic ministry: "Then those from the peoples, tribes, tongues, and nations will see their dead bodies three-and-a-half days, and not allow their dead bodies to be put into graves" (Rev. 11:9). How could all nations see two bodies lying in the street of Jerusalem simultaneously? With the advent of cell phone technology, mobile TV and iPads, news can be watched live on our communication devices. What looked impossible before 1948 is now possible. Nations around the world can watch events unfolding at the same time, making the fulfillment of the prophecy of Revelation 11:9 possible.

Fourth Event: Development of Radio-Frequency Identification (1973-Present)

Radio-frequency identification (RFID) is the use of an object (typically referred to as an RFID tag) to track or identify a product, animal, or person using radio waves. This technology was patented in the United States in 1973 and is being developed for a wide range of applications, including medicine, banking, defense, communication, and public transport.

RFID is rapidly becoming commonplace for product identification. As warehousing and logistics become automated, it is also increasingly being used in manufacturing and distribution. What is really causing students of prophecy to pay attention is the fact that it is increasingly being used in people. In Spain, for example, an exclusive club has already experimented with this technology.

> The Baja Beach Club in Barcelona, Spain is the first business to use the VeriChip System to grant customers access to VIP areas and provide an easy payment option. Club patrons can have a rice grain-sized RFID device implanted in their hand or arm. Once the unique 10-digit identification number in the VeriChip device is entered into the system, the patron can pay for drinks with a wave of the hand.[2]

RFID technology will continue to be perfected. Among the possible applications is a microchip human implant that can be programmed to replace cash, credit, and debit cards. In the nearest future, possibly between 2018 and 2025, microchip human implant will become the acceptable form of payment in some countries, fulfilling the Word of God:

> He causes all, both small and great, rich and poor, free and slave, to receive a mark on their right hand or on their foreheads, and that no one may buy or sell except one who has the mark or the name of the beast, or the number of his name. (Rev. 13:16-17)

The supporters and promoters of microchip human implant will argue for its convenience and security—that it cannot be lost, stolen, or duplicated. Moreover, in the name of security and peace, cultural resistance to this form of invasive technology will be withered down.

Here is what I am convinced will be experienced by the church: Between 2015 and 2025, there will be a major breakthrough in biotechnology, a breakthrough that will bring prosperity and security to the United States,

---

[2] http://www.technovelgy.com/ct/Science-Fiction-News. asp?NewsNum=104 (last accessed June 21, 2012)

a breakthrough that will lead to mass production of microchips, a breakthrough that will change the face of the world financial system, forever creating a cashless society. This microchip will be implanted on the right hand, right arm, or forehead of people in the world. The world's highly placed governmental officials and corporate movers and shakers will receive their implants on their foreheads so that they can have access to special buildings and rooms with remote control doors. For most others, it will be implanted on the right hand or forearm. This implant will be done quickly and easily with a painless laser technology and be invisible to the naked eye. Hence, it will not appear like a birthmark or tattoo. It will only be read by special scanners. This will be used initially as an alternative to liquid cash, but gradually paper money will be phased out. This is what the Bible refers to as "the mark of the beast." *Do not take this mark.*

This is when the faith of many will be tested. Who are you going to worship? Money or the living God? What is the most important thing in your life? Money or the Word of God? Who are you going to obey? The world or the Word of God? Are you ready to forsake all things to gain Jesus Christ? Are you willing and ready to take the narrow path, knowing that broad is the way that leads to destruction? Where are you planning to spend your eternity, in heaven or in hell? Please pay attention to the Word of God regarding this strange phenomenon.

> Then a third angel followed them, saying with a loud voice, *"If anyone worships the beast and his image, and receives his mark on his forehead or on his hand, he himself shall also drink of the wine of the wrath of God, which is poured out full strength into the cup of his indignation.* He shall be tormented with fire and brimstone in the presence of the holy angels and in the presence of the Lamb" . . . Then I heard a voice from heaven saying to me, "Write: 'Blessed are the dead who die in the Lord from now on.'" "Yes," says the Spirit, "that

they may rest from their labors, and their works follow them." (Rev. 14:9-13, emphasis mine)

Blessed are the dead who die in the Lord from now on. This refers to everyone who pays the ultimate price in defense of their faith in Christ Jesus.

The wrath of God is coming upon the wicked of this world. However, according to the above passage, *the mark of the beast will precede the wrath of God.* The destruction of the twin cities of Sodom and Gomorrah in the Scriptures is a warning to this present generation that the living God will not allow evil to triumph. The seventh seal in a later chapter of this book describes in detail the coming wrath of God.

The future is here. The world is becoming a global village, and the Scripture is warning us to watch and pray. We need to stand firm in the Lord Jesus Christ so that if the Lord delays in his coming, we will be prepared not to receive this human implant into our right hands or foreheads because it is anti-God and anti-Christ.

Chapter Three

The Sign of the Six Days

From the day that Adam was thrown out of the garden of Eden, the process of restoring the human race into the kingdom of God began. Very soon it will be six thousand years since Adam was sent forth from the beautiful garden. This becomes significant when we understand it from the standpoint of the coming reign of Jesus Christ. According to the book of Revelation, Jesus Christ is coming to reign for one thousand years (this period is often called the millennial reign). Why one thousand years? Why not two thousand years? Why not three thousand years? What is the significance of one thousand? By saying that Jesus Christ is coming to reign for one thousand years, the Scripture is saying that Jesus Christ is going to reign for one day, the day that the Lord God would rest because Satan will be in bondage. (Rev. 20:1-2)

God's prophetic calendar for humanity was revealed during the creation of the world. According to the Word of God in Genesis 1 and 2, the heavens and the earth were created in six days, and on the seventh day, God rested.

We can see beautiful parallels here between the creation of the world and the salvation of humanity. It took six days to create the heavens and the earth, and it is taking six thousand years to restore humanity into the kingdom of God, a kingdom that is coming in the power and glory of God. Therefore, a day is like a thousand years. This principle is found in the prophecy of Peter regarding the last days:

> But, beloved, do not forget this one thing, that *with the Lord one day is as a thousand years*, and a thousand years as one day. The Lord is not slack concerning his promise, as some count slackness, but is longsuffering toward us, not willing that any should perish but that all should come to repentance. (2 Peter 3:8-9, emphasis mine)

Here the apostle Peter is describing the relationship between a day in the eyes of the Lord and a literal one thousand years. God is not slow but full of mercies and kindness. However, the promise of His coming will be fulfilled in the last days, also known as the time of the last generation. Since the rest of God in Genesis is compared to the coming kingdom of God, we can conclude that to enter into the kingdom of God is to enter into the rest of God.

To God be the glory! The chronology of the Bible from Adam to the building of the first temple in Jerusalem, known as Solomon's Temple, is evident from Scripture. A detailed calendar from the time that Adam left the garden of Eden, to the completion of the temple built by Solomon was preserved for us (See Appendix). Hence, we gain insight into the time we are in and are better able to appreciate the reality of the last days as predicted by God's prophets. Knowing that we are at the tail end of the sixth millennium from Adam means that the beginning of the seventh millennium (which will usher in the reign of Christ), is at hand.

When Is the End of the Six Thousand Years?

Studies of the chronology of generations in Genesis place the creation of Adam in 3975 B.C.[3] (See Appendix). If three thousand years from Adam ended in 975 B.C., when is four thousand years going to end? The answer is 975 B.C. +

---

[3]   Frank R. Klassen, *The Chronology of the Bible* (Nashville, TN: Regal Publishers, 1975), 6. Detailed discussion of this topic can be found in Appendix A.

1,000 years = 26 A.D. Why not 25 AD? Since there is no 0 B.C. or 0 A.D., we jump from 1 B.C to 1 A.D., thereby gaining one year. Hence we end up with 26 A.D.

If four thousand years from Adam ended in 26 A.D., when is five thousand years going to end? The answer is 26 A.D. + 1,000 years = 1026 A.D. If five thousand years from Adam ended in 1026 A.D., when is six thousand years going to end? The answer is 1026 A.D. + 1,000 years = 2026 A.D.

Therefore:

- The biblical four thousand years ended in 26 A.D. (975 B.C. + 1,000 years).
- The biblical five thousand years ended in 1026 A.D. (26 A.D. + 1,000 years).
- The biblical six thousand years will end in 2026 A.D. (1026 A.D. + 1,000 years).

Using literal dates from the Scriptures, the present millennium is going to end in 2026 A.D. Since three thousand years from Adam was significantly related to the building of the first temple in Jerusalem (See Appendix), six thousand years from Adam may be related to a major end-time event, which is the building of a new temple in Jerusalem. This temple, which is being referred to as "the third temple" is alluded to throughout the end-time Scriptures (including Daniel 9:27, Matthew 24:15, and 2 Thessalonians 2:3-4)

Moreover, it is important to note that 2026 A.D. falls in the middle of a very significant seven-year period spanning 2022-2029 A.D. This seven-year period will be discussed in detail when we get to the fifth seal. *What we need to remember for now is that 2026 A.D., not 2000 A.D., marks the six thousandth year from the time of Adam.*

Chapter Four

Sign of the Year of Jubilee

From Scripture, we are able to see a clear record of the timeline from Adam to the exodus from Egypt. According to this record, the exodus of the children of Israel took place exactly 2513 years from Adam, which is equal to 1462 B.C. In 1422 B.C., the Hebrews entered the Promised Land. Seven years later, they celebrated the Sabbath year. Fifty years after that, they celebrated the Jubilee in the Promised Land, according to the commandment of God.

In this chapter, we will look at biblical references concerning the Sabbath year, how seven Sabbath years make up a Jubilee, and the significance of forty Jubilees in God's relationship with the human race.

The Sabbath Year

According to the Word of God, the Jews were required to set apart every seventh year, known as the Sabbath year, to rest, rejoice, and worship God.

> Six years you shall sow your field, and six years you shall prune your vineyard, and gather its fruit; but in the seventh year there shall be a Sabbath of solemn rest for the land, a Sabbath to the Lord. You shall neither sow your field nor prune your vineyard. (Lev. 25:3-4)

In this chapter, we will trace the Sabbath year from the first day that the Jews entered the Promised Land and see how this is related to end-time events. First we need to understand the relationship between Jewish calendar and our modern-day calendar.

Jewish Calendar	Modern Calendar
1st Month	March/April
2nd Month	April/May
3rd Month	May/June
4th Month	June/July
5th Month	July/August
6th Month	August/September
7th Month	September/October
8th Month	October/November
9th Month	November/December
10th Month	December/January
11th Month	January/February
12th Month	February/March

Since the Sabbath year always starts in the seventh month of the Jewish calendar, the Sabbath year always starts in September/October of the modern calendar.

Now something very significant must be done at the beginning of each Sabbath year. According to Moses, the book of the law must be read during the Feast of Tabernacle (i.e., from the fourteenth to the twenty-first day of the seventh month). An understanding of this reading will enable us identify the last recorded Sabbath year in the Scripture.

> And Moses commanded them, saying: "*At the end of every seven years,* at the appointed time in the year of release, at the Feast of Tabernacles, when all Israel comes to appear before the Lord your God in the place which he chooses, you shall read this law before all Israel in their hearing." (Deut. 31:9-11, emphasis mine)

This instruction is pivotal. It gives a clear conception of the last Sabbath year recorded in the Scripture, and it was well documented by Jewish historians. The last recorded Sabbath year was led by Ezra, who was both a priest and a scribe, in the seventh year of King Artaxerxes, king of Persia. (Ezra 7:6-8)

Last Recorded Sabbath Year in the Bible— 458 B.C.

Artaxerxes I was king of the Persian Empire from 465-424 B.C. Therefore, the seventh year of Artaxerxes would have been 458 B.C.[4] In September/October 458 B.C., Ezra celebrated the beginning of a Sabbath year on the first day of the Jewish seventh month. He read from the book of the law in the hearing of all the people. (Neh. 8: 1-2; 17-18)

See Table 2 on the dates of Sabbath years from 773-458 B.C. in the latter part of this chapter.

Year of Jubilee

According to the Word of God, the Jews were required to set apart every fiftieth year to declare freedom in all their land. This is known as the Year of Jubilee or the year of the Lord.

> And you shall count seven Sabbaths of years for yourself, seven times seven years; and the time of the seven Sabbaths of years shall be to you forty-nine years. Then you shall cause the trumpet of the Jubilee to sound on the tenth day of the seventh month; on the Day of Atonement you shall make the trumpet to sound throughout all your land. And you shall consecrate the fiftieth year, and proclaim liberty throughout all the land to all its inhabitants. It shall be a Jubilee for you;

---

[4]   http://en.wikipedia.org/wiki/Artaxerxes (last accessed June 21, 2012)

and each of you shall return to his possession,
and each of you shall return to his family. (Lev.
25:8-10, emphasis mine)

Every fiftieth year from the first day the Jews stepped into
the Promised Land was set apart for great rejoicing and
celebration. It was designed to be a year of new beginnings.
Debts were cancelled and Jewish slaves were released. In
contemporary times, the Year of Jubilee would be when
mortgages, auto loans, student loans, and credit card
debts were cancelled. Therefore creditors would give loans
based on the timeline of each Jubilee cycle—bigger loans
at the beginning of the cycle and lesser loans at the end.
This was designed by God to save the poor from their rich
oppressors. (Lev. 25:25-28)

The tenth day of the seventh month of every fiftieth year is
the beginning of a Year of Jubilee, a year of freedom, the
year of the Lord. Every forty-ninth year is a Sabbath year,
while every fiftieth year is a Year of Jubilee. The exodus of
the children of Israel from Egypt took place in the month of
Abib (April) 1462 B.C.[5] Forty years later, in April 1422 B.C.,
the children of Israel entered the Promised Land.

On April 1422 B.C., the children of Israel kept the first
Passover in the Promised Land. (Josh. 5:10)

If 1422 B.C. was the first year of the Jews in the Promised
Land, then the first Jubilee was proclaimed and celebrated
fifty years afterwards, on September/October 1372 B.C.
The table below shows the timetable of years of Jubilee
from that time to contemporary times. (even if the Jews
have not always observed them)

---

[5]   Appendix "Dating the Years from Adam"

TABLE ONE

Dates of Seventy Jubilees (Every Fiftieth Year)									
	Year B.C.		Year B.C.		Year A.D.		Year A.D.		Year A.D.
0	1422	15	672	29	29	13	679	27	1379
1	1372	16	622			14	729	28	1429
2	1322	17	572	1	79	15	779	29	1479
3	1272	18	522	2	129	16	829	30	1529
4	1222	19	472	3	179	17	879	31	1579
5	1172	20	422	4	229	18	929	32	1629
6	1122	21	372	5	279	19	979	33	1679
7	1072	22	322	6	329	20	1029	34	1729
8	1022	23	272	7	379	21	1079	35	1779
9	972	24	222	8	429	22	1129	36	1829
10	922	25	172	9	479	23	1179	37	1879
11	872	26	122	10	529	24	1229	38	1929
12	822	27	72	11	579	25	1279	39	1979
13	772	28	22	12	629	26	1329	40	**2029**
14	722								

Seven Cycles of Sabbath Years = One Jubilee

Year of Jubilee	1st-7th Year =1st Sabbath Cycle	8th-14th Year = 2nd Sabbath Cycle	15th-21st Year = 3rd Sabbath Cycle	22nd-28th Year = 4th Sabbath Cycle	29th-35th Year = 5th Sabbath Cycle	36th-42nd Year = 6th Sabbath Cycle	43rd-49th Year = 7th Sabbath Cycle	Year of Jubilee

The above tables can be applied to our present-day calendar. Since the last Jubilee was in 1979, the next Jubilee will be in 2029 A.D. An understanding of this calendar is fundamental to understanding the seven seals of the book of Revelation. As discussed above, the Jewish New Year is marked by the celebration of the Feast of Trumpets, otherwise known as Rosh Hashanah. This feast is always celebrated around September or October of our modern calendar. Using available Jewish records, we can easily locate the Rosh Hashanahs from 1980-2029. The Sabbath cycles referred to below have been identified since 1980.

1979: Year of Jubilee

1980-1987	First Sabbath cycle, with September 1980 as the beginning of the cycle and October 1986 to September 1987 as the Sabbath year.
1987-1994	Second Sabbath cycle, with September 1987 as the beginning of the cycle and September 1993-1994 as the Sabbath year.
1994-2001	Third Sabbath cycle, with September 1994 as the beginning of the cycle and September 2000-2001 as the Sabbath year.
2001-2008	Fourth Sabbath cycle, with September 2001 as the beginning of the cycle and September 2007-2008 as the Sabbath year.
2008-2015	Fifth Sabbath cycle, with September 2008 as the beginning of the cycle and September 2014-2015 as the Sabbath year.
2015-2022	Sixth Sabbath cycle, with September 2015 as the beginning of the cycle and September 2021-2022 as the Sabbath year.
2022-2029	Seventh Sabbath cycle, with September 2022 as the beginning of the cycle and September 2028-2029 as the Sabbath year.
2029-2030 (Year of Jubilee)	This will start in **September 19, 2029 on Yom Kippur and end in October 6, 2030.**

The years 1993 A.D. and 2029 A.D. are very significant in this generation. According to present Jewish tradition (using every forty-ninth year as a Jubilee), 1993 A.D. is the fortieth Jubilee from the time of Christ (33 A.D.). In contrast, according to old Jewish tradition (kept now by Christians) using every fiftieth year as a Jubilee, 2029 A.D. is the fortieth Jubilee from the time of Christ. (29 A.D.)

NOTE: The years 1994, 2001, 2008, 2015, 2022, and 2029 are very significant years in God's end-time timetable. The primary purpose of this book is to help God's people understand that those years are related to the seven seals of Revelation and to encourage them to pay attention to the current affairs in our world as they relate to these dates. We need to watch and pray, but how do we watch if we do not know what to watch for? How do we prepare if we cannot see the signs of His coming?

The Last Five Sabbath Cycles

1994-	2001-	2008-	2015-	2022-
2001	2008	2015	2022	2029

Knowing that 1994, 2001, 2008, 2015, 2022, and 2029 mark the beginning of each seven-year Sabbath cycle, we can now link those years with the seven seals of Revelation.

    1994-2001 = first seal
    2001-2008 = second seal
    2008-2015 = third seal
    2015-2022 = fourth seal
    2022-2029 = fifth seal
    2029-2030 = the Year of Jubilee
    2030-2037 = sixth seal
    2030-2037 = seventh seal

Note that the sixth and seventh seals run concurrently. The sixth seal describes heavenly events from the time of the rapture. The seventh seal describes the earthly manifestation of the wrath of God on those who are left behind after the rapture. Therefore, the seven-year period of the marriage supper of the Lamb coincides with the seven-year period of the outpouring of the wrath of God on those who are left behind. One can either be in heaven (after being raptured by Jesus) celebrating one's victory over death or be left behind to experience the wrath of God on earth—hence the proposition that the sixth and the seventh seals take place at the same time.

Jesus Christ, Our Jubilee

The institution of the Year of Jubilee is a reference to the earthly ministry of our Lord Jesus Christ. Jubilee is associated with freedom, and the coming of Christ brought freedom. It sets people free from the oppression of the devil, disease, sin, and death. Jesus said, "So if the Son sets you free, you will be free indeed." (John 8:36)

Jubilee is a year of restoration. That is why Jesus is coming back to restore all things. Jesus is the restorer. He will usher in the societal utopia that has eluded the human race since the fall. Jubilee is also a reference to a new kind of government to be ushered in by Jesus Christ, the kingdom of God. This is the subjection of the human race to the kingly rule of God. According to Paul, this kingdom will bring justice, peace, and joy to all. (Rom. 14:17)

The Beginning of the Public Ministry of Christ

Jesus Christ started his earthly ministry on a day of Jubilee. Let me quickly elucidate. According to the Jubilee timetable presented here, the twenty-ninth Jubilee of the children of Israel in the Promised Land occurred in 29 A.D. This was the same year John the Baptist, the forerunner of Jesus Christ, began his ministry:

> Now in the fifteenth year of the reign of Tiberius Caesar . . . while Annas and Caiaphas were high priests, the word of God came to John the son of Zacharias in the wilderness. And he went into all

the region around the Jordan, preaching a baptism of repentance for the remission of sins. (Luke 3:1-3)

When was the fifteenth year of the reign of Tiberius Caesar? Tiberius Julius Caesar Augustus, born Tiberius Claudius Nero (November 16, 42 B.C. to March 16, A.D. 37), was the second Roman emperor from the death of Augustus in A.D. 14 until his death in 37 A.D.[6] If Tiberius Caesar became emperor in 14 A.D., the fifteenth year of his reign would have been 29 A.D. Therefore, John the Baptist started his ministry in 29 A.D. We know from the Scriptures that John the Baptist was six months older than Jesus Christ. Six months after he announced the birth of John, the angel Gabriel was sent to Mary. (Luke 1:26-27)

Six months after the beginning of John's ministry, Jesus started his public ministry: "Now Jesus himself began his ministry at about thirty years of age" (Luke 3:23). This implies that Jesus and John (his forerunner) were both thirty years old when they started their ministries. John started his preaching in the spring of the 29 A.D. and Jesus followed six months later in the autumn/fall.

In September/October 29 A.D., on the tenth day of the month (which should have been the Day of Atonement), the day the Year of Jubilee would have been proclaimed, Jesus entered the temple, and as the Lord of Jubilee, proclaimed the Lord's year:

> "The Spirit of the Lord is upon me, because he has anointed me to preach the gospel to the poor; he has sent me to heal the brokenhearted, to proclaim liberty to the captives and recovery of sight to the blind, to set at liberty those who are oppressed; to proclaim the acceptable year of the Lord." . . . "Today this Scripture is fulfilled in your hearing." (Luke 4:18-21)

---

[6]   http://en.wikipedia.org/wiki/Tiberius (last accessed June 21, 2012)

Jesus proclaimed and celebrated the twenty-ninth Jubilee in 29 A.D. He declared without ambiguity or equivocation that what Isaiah prophesied was in motion. Scripture was being fulfilled right before the people's eyes!

Significance of Forty Jubilees (Two Thousand Years)

What is the length of forty Jubilees if a Jubilee occurs every fifty years? The answer is 40 x 50 = 2,000 years. Forty Jubilees equals two thousand years. We must have this at the back of our mind if we want to have a lucid understanding of God's timetable.

We know that from Adam to Abraham was two thousand years. To be exact, it was from the eighth year of Adam (3967 B.C.) to the birth of Abraham. (See Appendix) Therefore, from Adam to Abraham was forty Jubilees.

Eighth year of Adam (3967 B.C.)—birth of Abraham (1967 B.C.) = 2,000 years = 40 Jubilees.

Jesus Christ was crucified and resurrected in 33 A.D. How many years are there between 1967 B.C. and 33 A.D.? The answer is 2,000 years = 40 Jubilees. From Abraham to Jesus Christ = 40 Jubilees.

Birth of Abraham (1967 B.C.)—death and resurrection of Christ (33 A.D.) = 2000 years = 40 Jubilees

From Jesus Christ (29 A.D.) to the end of this present generation in 2029 A.D. will be two thousand years = 40 Jubilees

From Jesus Christ (29 A.D.) to Jubilee in 2029 A.D. = 40 Jubilees

Knowing that every fortieth Jubilee is very significant in God's timetable, the Holy Spirit is calling you to be ready for the marriage supper of the Lamb. The rapture and the second coming of Christ are close—at the door—and will be witnessed by many who are reading this book. In Revelation 22:12-13, Jesus said, "Behold, I am coming quickly, and my reward is with me, to give to every one according to his work. I am the Alpha and the Omega, the Beginning and the End, the First and the Last."

Jubilee Ceased

Unfortunately, the proclamation and celebration of Jubilee by the children of Israel ceased after the northern kingdom went into captivity in 720 B.C. The northern kingdom existed as an independent state until around 720 B.C. when it was conquered by the Assyrian Empire, according to some sources. The cut-off date was 720 B.C., after which there has been no documentation of Jubilee being celebrated. Many Jewish scholars posit that this is because many Jewish families were transplanted to Assyria; therefore, the Jubilee law was no longer applicable. Traditionally, lands were restored to Jewish families at each Jubilee, but this was impractical because the Assyrians were in control of the northern kingdom. Hence from 720 B.C. on, the celebration of Jubilee ceased.

By looking at the above dates of Jubilee, the fourteenth Jubilee, which came in 722 B.C., was not celebrated because the northern kingdom was fighting against the king of Assyria. The battle lasted for three years, from 723-720 B.C. (2Kings 18:9-11)

This means that the last Jubilee celebrated by the children of Israel was the thirteenth Jubilee in 772 B.C. Although Jubilee celebration ceased after 772 B.C., the Jews continued to be faithful with the documentation of the Sabbath years, with occasional celebration during waves of national revivals. If Jubilee was in 772 B.C., then the prior Sabbath year would have been 773 B.C. If 773 B.C. was a Sabbath year, then we can determine whether Ezra's celebration of the Sabbath year in 458 B.C. was accurate.

With the cessation of Jubilee, Jewish religious leaders continued to count only the Sabbath years.

Ezra Celebrated the Sabbath Year

From the destruction of the northern kingdom through the Babylonian captivity of the southern kingdom until the time of Ezra, the celebration of Sabbath years was not recorded in the Scriptures. Ezra, a Babylonian Jew who led a group of Jews from Babylon back to Jerusalem, was used by God to bring about national revival. He ensured that the religion of the returning Jews was in line with the Law of Moses. (Ezra 7:11-13)

> And Ezra came to Jerusalem in the fifth month, which was in the seventh year of the king . . . (Ezra 7:8)

This passage shows that Ezra came to Jerusalem in the seventh year of King Artaxerxes. Artaxerxes I is recorded as being king of the Persian Empire from 465-424 B.C.[7] Therefore, the seventh year of Artaxerxes I would have been 458 B.C. In September/October 458 B.C., Ezra celebrated the beginning of a Sabbath year. The table below confirms that Ezra was correct in choosing 458 B.C. as a Sabbath year.

772 B.C. was the thirteenth Jubilee of the children of Israel in the Promised Land. Since we know that every Jubilee is preceded by a Sabbath year, this tells us that the Sabbath year immediately prior to this particular Jubilee would have been 773 B.C. The table below shows all the dates of Sabbath years from 773-458 B.C.

---

[7]   http://en.wikipedia.org/wiki/Artaxerxes (last accessed June 21, 2012)

Table Two: Dates of Sabbath Years From 773-458 B.C.

	Year B.C.		Year B.C.		Year B.C.		Year B.C.
1	773	13	689	25	605	37	521
2	766	14	682	26	598	38	514
3	759	15	675	27	591	39	507
4	752	16	668	28	584	40	500
5	745	17	661	29	577	41	493
6	738	18	654	30	570	42	486
7	731	19	647	31	563	43	479
8	724	20	640	32	556	44	472
9	717	21	633	33	549	45	465
10	710	22	626	34	542	46	458
11	703	23	619	35	535		
12	696	24	612	36	528		

Jubilee Timetable Revised

From the time of Ezra in 458 B.C. until now, the Jews have been faithful in documenting every seventh year as a Sabbath year. From the time that Jubilee celebration ceased, every forty-ninth year, rather than every fiftieth year, became the acceptable date of Jubilee. From 458 B.C. on, every forty-ninth year was accepted as a Jubilee year. This is still being practiced today.

In order to have a better understanding of the impact of this revolution in the documentation of the Year of Jubilee, let us revise the dates of Jubilee to reflect the present-day practice of the Jews. This revision would show that from the time of Ezra, Jubilee was documented by Jewish religious leaders as occurring every forty-ninth year.

Dates of Jubilees (Every Forty-Ninth Year From Ezra)

	Year B.C.		Year A.D.		Year A.D.		Year A.D.
0	458	10	33	14	719	28	1405
1	409	1	82	15	768	29	1454
2	360	2	131	16	817	30	1503
3	311	3	180	17	866	31	1552
4	262	4	229	18	915	32	1601
5	213	5	278	19	964	33	1650
6	164	6	327	20	1013	34	1699
7	115	7	376	21	1062	35	1748
8	66	8	425	22	1111	36	1797
9	17	9	474	23	1160	37	1846
		10	523	24	1209	38	1895
		11	572	25	1258	39	1944
		12	621	26	1307	40	1993
		13	670	27	1356		

This table shows why many Bible and Jewish scholars chose 1993/4 as the Year of Jubilee. This is obtained by using present Jewish tradition to calculate the Jubilee years—that is, every forty-ninth year from the time of Ezra. This tradition shows 33 A.D., the year of the death and resurrection of Jesus Christ, as a Jubilee year.

The years 1993 A.D. and 2029 A.D. are very significant in this generation. According to present Jewish tradition (using every forty-ninth year as a Jubilee), 1993 A.D. is the fortieth Jubilee from the time of Christ (33 A.D.). In contrast, according to old Jewish tradition (kept now by Christians) using every fiftieth year as a Jubilee, 2029 A.D. is the fortieth Jubilee from the time of Christ (29 A.D.). *Between 1993 and 2029 A.D., the first through the last seals of the book of Revelation are being opened.* From 1993-2029 A.D. are five Sabbath cycles that correspond to the first five seals of the book of Revelation.

These five Sabbath cycles are very significant to end-time events and our understanding of the book of Revelation. Jesus has revealed to us the events that will happen during the end times, and we need to pay attention.

Here are the seven seals and their timelines using the sabbatical cycles between 1993-2029 A.D. These seven seals will be discussed in detail in the latter part of this book. They are introduced here only to illustrate the significance of sabbatical cycles.

The first seal (September 1994-2001): global move for peace

> Now I saw when the Lamb opened one of the seals; and I heard one of the four living creatures saying with a voice like thunder, "Come and see." And I looked, and behold, a white horse. He who sat on it had a bow; and a crown was given to him, and he went out conquering and to conquer. (Rev. 6:1-2)

The second seal (September 2001-2008): global war against terrorism

> When he opened the second seal, I heard the second living creature saying, "Come and see." Another horse, fiery red, went out. And it was granted to the one who sat on it to take peace from the earth, and that people should kill one another; and there was given to him a great sword. (Rev. 6:3-4)

The third seal (September 2008-2015): global economic depression and hyper-inflation

> When he opened the third seal, I heard the third living creature say, "Come and see." So I looked, and behold, a black horse, and he who sat on it had a pair of scales in his hand. And I heard a

voice in the midst of the four living creatures saying, "A quart of wheat for a denarius, and three quarts of barley for a denarius; and do not harm the oil and the wine." (Rev. 6: 5-6)

The fourth seal (September 2015-2022): World War III

When he opened the fourth seal, I heard the voice of the fourth living creature saying, "Come and see." So I looked, and behold, a pale horse. And the name of him who sat on it was Death, and Hades followed with him. And power was given to them over a fourth of the earth, to kill with sword, with hunger, with death, and by the beasts of the earth. (Rev. 6:7-8)

The fifth seal (September 2022-2029): severe persecution of the saints and the great tribulation of the Jews

When he opened the fifth seal, I saw under the altar the souls of those who had been slain for the word of God and for the testimony which they held. And they cried with a loud voice, saying, "How long, O Lord, holy and true, until you judge and avenge our blood on those who dwell on the earth?" Then a white robe was given to each of them; and it was said to them that they should rest a little while longer, until both the number of their fellow servants and their brethren, who would be killed as they were, was completed. (Rev. 6:9-11)

The sixth seal (September 2029-2037): the rapture of the saints and the marriage supper of the lamb

I looked when he opened the sixth seal, and behold, there was a great earthquake; and the sun became black as sackcloth of hair, and the moon became like blood. And the stars of heaven fell to the earth, as a fig tree drops its late figs when it is shaken by a mighty wind. Then the sky receded as a scroll when it is rolled up, and every mountain and island was moved out of its place. (Rev. 6:12-14)

After these things I looked, and behold, a great multitude which no one could number, of all nations, tribes, peoples, and tongues, standing before the throne and before the Lamb, clothed with white robes, with palm branches in their hands, and crying out with a loud voice, saying, "Salvation belongs to our God who sits on the throne, and to the Lamb!" (Rev. 7:9-10)

The seventh seal (September 2029-2037): the wrath of God on those left behind

The sixth and seventh seals run concurrently. The seventh seal is the seven trumpets of the wrath of God described in Revelation 8 and 9. While the marriage supper of the Lamb is taking place in heaven, the wrath of God is being poured on those who are left behind.

The Next Jubilee

If the coming of the Lord Jesus Christ is delayed, the next Jubilee celebration by Christians will start on September 19, 2029 and end on October 6, 2030. This shows how close we are to the end of this generation. *Our Lord Jesus Christ may come before or after the coming Jubilee celebration. Let us therefore be ready for the coming bridegroom.*

As we press forward through these perilous times, we need to walk with the understanding that the Jubilee represents freedom from death, disease, debt, slavery, oppression, trials, tribulations, and persecution. The celebration of Jubilee is the victory of life over death, the victory of righteousness over sin, and the victory of the kingdom of God over the kingdom of darkness. This future Jubilee also represents the end of the forty-two months (three-and-one-half years, or 1260 days) of the great tribulation of the elect.

Chapter Five

First, Second, and Third Seals

The First Seal: NATO for Peace (September 1994-2001)

First Event: False Christ/ False Peace	First Seal: False Christ/ False Peace
And Jesus answered and said to them: "Take heed that no one deceives you. For many will come in my name, saying, 'I am the Christ,' and will deceive many." (Matt. 24:4-5)	Now I saw when the Lamb opened one of the seals; and I heard one of the four living creatures saying with a voice like thunder, "Come and see." And I looked, and behold, a white horse. He who sat on it had a bow; and a crown was given to him, and he went out conquering and to conquer. (Rev. 6:1-2)

In the parallel passages above, we see Jesus and the apostle John describing the same time period, the first seal. The rider on the white horse represents peace, yet he is equipped to make war in the name of peace. In fact, this is an attempt by man to bring about peace through human effort. This is a global movement. The phrase "the rider went out conquering and to conquer" shows that peace will be sustained by force during this period.

It is interesting to note that world peace was sustained by NATO between 1994 and 2001. It is on record that something historic happened on September 12, 1994. According to an article written by Dean Murphy in the *Los Angeles Times* on the same day, U.S. soldiers joined others from twelve European countries to hold a military exercise in Poland, an exercise that has been referred to as historic in post-cold War cooperation.

The success of NATO and the movement for global peace between 1994 and 2001 is well documented. According to one article,

> Between 1994 and 1997, wider forums for regional cooperation between NATO and its neighbors were set up, like the Partnership for Peace, the Mediterranean Dialogue Initiative and the Euro-Atlantic Partnership Council. On July 8, 1997, three former communist countries, Hungary, the Czech Republic, and Poland, were invited to join NATO, which finally happened in 1999. In 1998, the NATO-Russia Permanent Joint Council was established. On March 24, 1999, NATO saw its first broad-scale military engagement in the Kosovo War. This was an 11-week bombing campaign (which NATO called Operation Allied Force) against what was then the Federal Republic of Yugoslavia, in an effort to stop a Serbian-led crackdown on Albanian civilians in Kosovo. In August-September 2001, the alliance also mounted Operation Essential Harvest, a mission disarming ethnic Albanian militias in the Republic of Macedonia.[8]

The spiritual activities of the rider of the first seal were manifested on earth for seven years, from September 1994-2001. This was when NATO built up the most powerful military alliance in the world and continued to use war to propagate peace.

---

[8]   http://en.wikipedia.org/wiki/NATO (last accessed June 21, 2012)

Second Seal: Global Act of Terrorism (September 2001-2008)

Second Event: Peace Is Taken from the Earth	Second Seal: Peace Is Taken from the Earth
"And you will hear of wars and rumors of wars. See that you are not troubled; for all these things must come to pass, but the end is not yet." (Matt. 24:6, emphasis mine)	When he opened the second seal, I heard the second living creature saying, "Come and see." Another horse, fiery red, went out. *And it was granted to the one who sat on it to take peace from the earth, and that people should kill one another; and there was given to him a great sword.* (Rev. 6:3-4, emphasis mine)

The assignment of the second rider on the red horse is very clear—to take peace from the earth. Peace that had been achieved between 1994 and 2001 must be taken away by the rider of this horse. Subsequently, situations will be created to make *people kill one another.* This was what happened on September 11, 2001. In one day, the global peace movement was terminated. On that day, terrorists successfully hijacked airplanes in the United States and destroyed the Twin Towers of the World Trade Center. In that attack on U.S. soil, thousands lost their lives. Even the Pentagon, the headquarters of the U.S. Department of Defense, was hit. What wickedness! That incident was the death knell for the growing movement for global peace. It signaled the beginning of war.

In response, the United States declared war on Afghanistan on October 7, 2001. The reason was twofold: to decimate Al-Qaeda in that country and to oust the Taliban, the fundamentalist Islamic militia ruling Afghanistan and sympathetic to Al-Qaeda.

As part of its war against terrorism, the United States also invaded Iraq. This decision was made on the assumption that the late President Saddam Hussein had weapons of mass destruction and was sympathetic to Al-Qaeda. Unfortunately, there was no evidence that Iraq actually stockpiled weapons of mass destruction, and its link to Al-Qaeda was not established.

The human cost of Iraqi war had been great. *The Lancet*, one of the oldest scientific medical journals in the world, in a survey published on October 11, 2006, estimated 654,965 excess deaths related to the war.[9] At the time, more than 12,000 casualties had been documented in Afghanistan alone.[10]

Since September 11, 2001, the number of terrorist attacks has skyrocketed—far too many to list. There have been attacks in Colombia, the Philippines, Indonesia, Kenya, Morocco, Thailand, Lebanon, Australia, Jordan, Nigeria, and other nations across the globe.

By paying attention to the Scriptures, we know that it is not going to get better. Rather, it is going to become worse until Jesus comes to reign. That is why this book is in your hands—to prepare you for these perilous times. This is also the time for the army of God to roll out with the message of God's kingdom that deliverance from the wrath to come can only be found in Christ Jesus.

Terrorism must be seen for what it really is—the physical manifestation of a war raging in the heavenlies for the souls of men. We must see these terrorists (men and women who have sworn their lives to martyrdom), as those Satan wants to destroy at all cost. That is why Christians must arise and shod their feet with the preparation of the gospel of peace

---

[9] http://en.wikipedia.org/wiki/Lancet_surveys_of_Iraq_War_casualties (last accessed June 21, 2012)

[10] http://en.wikipedia.org/wiki/List_of_civilian_casualties_of_the_War_in_Afghanistan_(2001%E2%80%93present) (last accessed June 21, 2012)

so that these people can be translated from the domain of darkness into the kingdom of God's Son, Jesus Christ.

The Third Seal: Global Economic Meltdown (September 2008-2015)

Third Event: Global Economic Crisis	Third Seal: Global Economic Crisis
"And there will be *famines*, pestilences, and earthquakes in various places." (Matt. 24:7, emphasis mine)	When he opened the third seal, I heard the third living creature say, "Come and see." *So I looked, and behold, a black horse, and he who sat on it had a pair of scales in his hand.* And I heard a voice in the midst of the four living creatures saying, "A quart of wheat for a denarius, and three quarts of barley for a denarius; and do not harm the oil and the wine." (Rev. 6:5-6)

The mandate of the third rider is to bring about famine in the world. He has a pair of scales in his hand, signifying global economic depression. In biblical times, eight measures of wheat were sold for a penny and twenty-four measures of barley were sold for a penny. During this future famine, only one measure of wheat or three measures of barley will be purchased for a penny. This means that food will be eight times its normal price[11]. *There will be economic depression followed by inflation to hyperinflation during this seven-year period.*

On Friday September 14, 2008, the economic crisis in the United States of America (U.S.A) was triggered by the Lehman Brothers, a big financial institution in the United States that filed for bankruptcy after the Federal

---

[11] Dake's*Annotated Reference Bible Commentary on Revelation* 6:5-6.

Reserve Bank refused to bail it out. Things became complicated when the Bank of America came out the same day to announce that it would be acquiring the financial institution, Merrill Lynch. There was panic in the market. The stock market crashed, capital froze, and uncertainty prevailed. The U.S. housing market bubble burst. The global economic crisis came uninvited. This happened exactly *seven years* after the advent of the global war on terrorism.

From September 2008-2015, I believe the ongoing global economic crisis will continue. During this period, many countries will continue to devalue their currencies, increase taxes, and address budget deficits in order to survive. Entitlement and welfare programs will continue to be curtailed. Decisions taken to solve the problem will split many nations into camps.

Personal Insight

In this and later sections of this book, I want to take the time to offer what I believe to be very likely scenarios that will play out related to each of the prophecies given to us in the book of Revelation. We will start with the seals.

Major Crisis in United States: In the United States, many people will be outraged, demanding solutions from their government to no avail. Militant militias will declare war on government agents. Foreign investors will clamor for what is their own. It will be a time of great confusion. The United States will continue to play a significant role in the global economic depression. Many prescribed solutions will fail. Many more banks will be closed down. Clouds of judgment are gathering over the United States.

If as a nation we refuse to repent of our greed, pride, moral degeneracy, exaltation of secular humanism over the knowledge of God, and exportation of pornography, God will allow the nation to be shaken.

Civil Unrest in the United States: After a presidential election sometime in the future, crisis will ensue and many cities will be thrown into turmoil. It will be a time of great upheaval. Civil unrest will be highly explosive, and the period will be traumatic. From the Southern and Midwestern parts of the United States, angry voices will be heard challenging the government. From coast to coast, many will agitate for the Constitution to be changed. Why? Because of their hidden agenda.

There will be a serious attempt by a single group of people to exercise absolute control over the entire nation. One or more states of the union will make an attempt to secede. There will be a big question mark on the word "united." In certain cities, there will be a great uprising against Muslims, and mosques will be burned. There will be an attempt by some to stoke the embers of racism in order to turn the crisis racially incendiary. If this succeeds, the conflagration will become worse. Armed militia, sponsored by few of the rich, will fight against government agents. Common sense will be thrown to the wind. Machine guns will be freely used in the streets.

Within two decades, very rapid changes will take place. Even the system of electing the president of the United States may change because of certain fundamental changes made to the Constitution. The right of citizens to own and bear arms will be taken away through constitutional amendment.

This is the time to call for prayer and fasting nationwide. The clouds of judgment over this great nation are not cast in stone. Judgment may or may not come. National response to divine warning will be the deciding factor. This is the time to bring men and women of God to the White House for intercessory prayers. All official representatives of the government from the county to federal levels must be involved.

The Great Depression: In an attempt to stimulate the economy, the U.S. government will spend so much that the nation's debt will become a source of great concern. Some top manipulators will siphon billions of dollars from the stock market and precipitate a fall. Trillions of dollars will be lost. There will be panic in the market because the Dow Jones Average will crash. Due to panic, many will sell their stocks to buy gold and silver to protect their assets. *The price of gold and silver will continue to soar. Those who are obedient to the voice of the Lord will protect their God-given wealth in the form of gold and silver.*

Civil War Is Coming to South Africa: Sequel to global economic depression, the South African economy, the largest economy in Africa, will be severely affected. Hence, after the glorious exit of Nelson Mandela, big labor unions will call for a labor strike to protest labor wages. This strike will be hijacked by people with hidden agendas to precipitate great civil unrest and civil war. South Africa will be divided. However, what is meant for evil will be turned into good by our Lord Jesus Christ, for in certain regions of South Africa, many Europeans, Christians, and Jews running from wars and tribulation will find refuge.

Devaluation of the U.S. Dollar: A time is coming when the *U.S. dollar will be worthless.* This will be the fulfillment of the Word of God in Revelation 6:6: "And I heard a voice in the midst of the four living creatures saying, 'A measure of wheat for a penny, and three measures of barley for a penny; and do not harm the oil and the wine.'"

There will be hyperinflation. People will not be interested in worthless paper money. Their trust will be in gold and silver.

Prices of goods and services will inflate out of control. Children will be starving on the streets of many nations. Many people will say, "How can these things happen to our beloved nation?" It will happen because nations have turned away from the true God.

Shockwaves of what is happening in the United States will be felt around the world. What happens in the United

States will affect financial institutions on a global basis. Leaders will be disgraced out of office. People will become confused and disoriented. Many will commit suicide. America will survive as a nation, but many people in power will be broken.

Fervent Prayers: The people of God will arise and pray in the coming crisis. They will pray fervently for deliverance and God's mercy. They will pray everywhere—in private and in public. Prayers will even be made in the Capitol. As a result, the Lord will intervene, and calm will come upon the nation. There will be an awesome display of the power and glory of God in the land. Let us therefore respond to the call to repentance. If we continue in sin, hoping that grace will abound, a greater judgment will come upon us.

A New Currency—A New World Order: A new currency will arise in the United States out of the ashes of the old. Debts will be wiped out in a single day. This will push the United States into a new order. Money from all over the world will be exchanged for this new currency, and the nation will flourish. A loose union of the United States, Canada, and Mexico will be formed and the new currency will be the legal tender. This will be the last empire to be formed in these last days. Eventually, this united triumvirate of economies will be merged with that of the whole European Union to create a *super economy* in preparation for a world currency. In the nearest future, there will be a world currency in place of the current U.S. dollar.

The European Union: It shall come to pass that the whole of Europe will experience civil unrest. This will be due to economic crisis and terrorist activities. The great Christian nations in Europe—Italy, France, and Britain—will begin to feel the wrath of the devil. There will be a resurrection of old land disputes and the redistribution of resources. There will be distrust among European leaders, and socialism will rise once again. Mainline churches will begin to use the political power of the state to oppress and suppress other growing Christian groups. There will be an emergence of new political leaders whose philosophical and ideological views are a threat to the conservative Christians in Europe. This will cause conflict to flare up between Northern Ireland and the United Kingdom until Northern Ireland is united with the Republic of Ireland to produce a United Ireland. This will pit the Catholic Church and the Church of England against each other, and it will be bloody. During that time, the Pope and the King of England will be in grave danger. The youths in these countries will become restless, and many will be manipulated into joining the military. Europe will be engulfed in conflict, but the greatest will be the invasion of Europe by the Russian armed forces after its failed attempt to invade Israel.

Creation of a Palestinian State: It shall come to pass that the Palestinian state will be created. This will be accomplished by dividing the land God gave Abraham and his descendants, thereby incurring his wrath:

> "For behold, in those days and at that time, *when I bring back the captives of Judah and Jerusalem,* I will also gather all nations, and bring them down to the Valley of Jehoshaphat; and I will enter into judgment with them there on account of my people, my heritage Israel, whom they have scattered among the nations; *they have also divided up my land.*" (Joel 3:1-2, emphasis mine)

The fulfillment of the prophecy to bring back the captives of Judah and Jerusalem occurred in 1948 when the Jews were brought back to their land. The second half of the prophecy will be fulfilled when the Palestinian state is created. Nations angling for the creation of such a state should pay attention to this prophecy. According to Joel, God's anger will wax hot and all the nations involved in dividing the land will be judged.

Iran, a Nuclear Nation: Iran will have weapons of mass destruction. Every form of diplomacy or sanction to stop this from occurring will fail. Some of those weapons will be smuggled to Libya, Syria, and Lebanon. This implies that

Israel will be surrounded by countries with weapons of mass destruction.

Vision of the Woman in a Basket

Zechariah 5:7-8, says a woman is seated in the midst of the flying container that is *secured by a talent of lead, and the name of the woman is wickedness.* There is a translation problem in these two verses that is relevant here and addressed by Michael Rood, a Hebrew author of the book, *The Mystery of Iniquity.* According to Rood, "the word *'Aisha'* in Hebrew means *fire offering,* whereas, the word *'Isha'* means *woman. 'Aisha' and 'Isha'* have the same consonants in the Hebrew language. Since vowels are not included in the original Hebrew texts, the context determines the meaning. Hence, the same word can be translated as *"woman"* or *"offering fire."*[12] By inserting "fire" in place of "woman" in the above passage, this is how it reads:

> "So I asked, 'What is it?' And he said, 'It is a *container* that is going forth.' He also said, 'This is their resemblance throughout the earth: Here is a lead disc lifted up, and this is a *fire* sitting inside the container'; then he said, 'This is Wickedness!' And he thrust it down into the *container, and threw the lead cover over its mouth.* Then I raised my eyes and looked, and there were *two fires,* coming with the wind in their wings; for they had wings like the wings of a stork, and they lifted up the *container* between earth and heaven." (Zech 5:6-9, emphasis mine)

According to this vision, a missile fitted with a nuclear warhead is carrying fire—destructive fire! That's why it was aptly labeled "wickedness" by the angel. Uranium for nuclear warheads is usually protected by thick lead

---

[12]   Michael Rood, *The Mystery of Iniquity* (Gainesville, FL: Bridge—Logos, 2001), 144.

in order to prevent contamination before detonation. Moreover, the propulsion of missiles by "two fires" coming from two short-side wings of the missiles is a common phenomenon.

As I round up this analysis of Zechariah's prophecy, let us check out what was said in verses 8-9:

> So I said to the angel who talked with me, "Where are they carrying the container?" And he said to me, "To build a house for it in the land of Shinar; when it is ready, the container will be set there on its base."

This is very instructive because this may happen within the next decade. There will be facilities for nuclear weaponry in the land of Shinar, which is comprised of Iraq, Iran, Syria, Jordan, Lebanon, and Saudi Arabia. Iran will trigger a nuclear weapon race in the Middle East.

All over the Middle East, especially in Iran, Syria, and Lebanon, thousands of missiles will have just one target— Israel. These missiles will be fitted with nuclear, biological, chemical, or conventional warheads. Nuclear weapons will be used in a great Middle East war, and Israel will be targeted. In this great war, Israel will be affected. Major Palestinian as well as Syrian cities will be destroyed.

Chapter Six

Fourth Seal Part 1: Middle East War (September 2015-2022)

Fourth Event: War	Fourth Seal: War
"For nation will rise against nation, and kingdom against kingdom . . . All these are the beginning of sorrows." (Matt. 24:7, 8)	When he opened the fourth seal, I heard the voice of the fourth living creature saying, "Come and see." So I looked, and behold, a pale horse. And the name of him who sat on it was Death, and Hades followed with him. And power was given to them over a fourth of the earth, to kill with sword, with hunger, with death, and by the beasts of the earth. (Rev. 6:7-8)

This war of the fourth seal shall involve one-fourth of the earth. By extrapolating from current world affairs, a possible scenario involves the United States, the European countries, Russia, Middle Eastern countries, and North African countries. The population of these countries is about one-fourth of the earth. Regardless of the nations involved, 25 percent of the world will be involved in this war.

This war will be related to four heavenly signs that we will now discuss. By heavenly sign, I mean lunar eclipse coinciding with the Jewish feasts of Passover and Tabernacles.

First Heavenly Sign: Tuesday, April 15, 2014— Passover Feast

According to NASA, there will be a total lunar eclipse on this day, and it will last approximately three hours and thirty-five minutes. The eclipse will be visible in Australia, the Pacific, and the Americas.[13] The Passover is celebrated to mark Israel's deliverance from bondage in Egypt. It is the first feast in the Hebrew religious calendar.

Second Heavenly Sign: Wednesday, October 8, 2014—Feast of Tabernacles

According to NASA, there will be a second total lunar eclipse on this day, and it will last for three hours and twenty minutes and will be visible in Asia, Australia, the Pacific and the Americas. Also known as Succoth, the Feast of Tabernacles begins on the eve of the fifteenth of Tishri (late September to late October) and is celebrated in commemoration of the shelter of the Israelites during their forty years in the wilderness. It is the last feast in the Hebrew religious calendar.

Third Heavenly Sign: Saturday, April 4, 2015— Passover Feast

According to NASA, there will be a third total lunar eclipse on this day, and it will last for three hours and twenty-nine minutes. It will be visible in Asia, Australia, the Pacific, and the Americas.

---

[13] http://eclipse.gsfc.nasa.gov/LEdecade/LEdecade2011.html (last accessed June 21, 2012)

Fourth Heavenly Sign: Monday, September 28, 2015—Feast of Tabernacles

According to NASA, there will be a fourth total lunar eclipse on this day, and it will last for three hours and twenty minutes. This eclipse will be visible in the East Pacific, the Americas, Europe, Africa, and West Asia.

These heavenly signs are important landmarks in God's prophetic calendar. A concatenation of four total lunar eclipses, all falling on God's appointed feast days (Passover and Tabernacles), is very significant. It is called a biblical tetrad.

Biblical Tetrad: Jewish Survival

A biblical tetrad is a very rare heavenly phenomenon. There were only two biblical tetrads in the last century, and both were very significant to the survival of Israel as a nation. The first was the 1949/50 tetrad and the second was the 1967/68 tetrad. There were no biblical tetrads for four hundred years prior to the one of 1949/50. There will be only one biblical tetrad in the twenty-first century, the 2014/2015 tetrad.

Biblical Tetrad: The Birth of Israel

On May 14, 1948, Israel became a nation. On May 15, 1948, her war with six Arab nations began. The war ended on January 7, 1949, and on the day of Passover, after their resettlement in their homeland, a biblical tetrad occurred. Here are the dates of the 1949/50 tetrad:

- Wednesday April 13, 1949: Feast of Passover (total lunar eclipse)
- Friday October 7,1949: Feast of Tabernacles (total lunar eclipse)

- Sunday April 2, 1950: Feast of Passover (total lunar eclipse)
- Tuesday September 26,1950: Feast of Tabernacles (total lunar eclipse)

Biblical Tetrad: The City of Jerusalem

The 1967/68 tetrad is related to Israel's battle for survival and the restoration of the city of Jerusalem. This six-day war with Egypt, Jordan, and Syria was fierce and decisive. The impact of the war is still being felt in these regions today. By the end of the war, Israel had gained control of the Sinai Peninsula, the Gaza Strip, the West Bank, East Jerusalem, and the Golan Heights.

After 1,890 years, Israel was finally in control of Jerusalem. Here are the dates of the 1967/1968 biblical tetrad:

- Monday April 24, 1967: Feast of Passover (total lunar eclipse)
- Wednesday October 18,1967: Feast of Tabernacles (total lunar eclipse)
- Saturday April 13, 1968: Feast of Passover (total lunar eclipse)
- Sunday October 6, 1968: Feast of Tabernacles (total lunar eclipse)

Biblical Tetrad: The Fourth Seal of the Book of Revelation

In the future, Israel's survival will once again be threatened by her neighbors in the Middle East. This is what the 2014/15 tetrad is all about. This coming Middle East crisis was described in detail by the prophet Ezekiel through the inspiration of the Holy Spirit. In this coming war, Israel will emerge victorious through divine intervention. An unexpected earthquake will not only discomfit the rampaging Russian army (as of today, officially the Armed

Forces of the Russian Federation) but also lead to the rebuilding of the third Jewish temple.

Interestingly, the 1949/50, 1967/68, and 2014/15 tetrads represent three stages of the end-time program of God.

- 1949/50 tetrad is related to the establishment of the state of Israel.
- 1967/68 tetrad is related to the city of Jerusalem coming under the control of Israel.
- 2014/2015 tetrad will relate to the survival of Israel and the building of the third temple in Jerusalem.

The Third Temple

Israel's first temple of worship was built in Jerusalem by King Solomon and completed in 975 B.C. (1 Kings 6:38)

For 389 years, the temple stood until it was destroyed by the Babylonians in 586 B.C. This occurred in the eleventh year of King Zedekiah. (1 Chron. 36:17-21)

When the Jewish exiles returned to Jerusalem after the completion of the seventy years, work on the second temple began. It was built on the Temple Mount, the same location as the first temple. Under the leadership of Governor Zerubbabel and the prophets Haggai and Zechariah, the second temple was completed in 516 B.C. (Ezra 6:14-15)

The second temple stood for 586 years until 70 A.D. when it was destroyed by Roman soldiers under the command of General Titus, who later became the Roman emperor. To date, the Jews have not been able to rebuild the temple. This is largely due to the fact that the Dome of the Rock, the oldest extant example of Islamic architecture, was built on the site 687-691 A.D., making it impossible for the Jews to rebuild on the same site.

Destruction of the Dome of Rock

Personal Insight: In the nearest future, God will cause a massive earthquake to shake the whole Temple Mount. In the process, the Dome of the Rock will be destroyed. This will make a way for the Jews to build the third temple, which will be done expeditiously under the leadership of prophets sent by God to help his people. Moreover, morning and evening sacrifices will be reinstituted and observed as they were in biblical times.

War in the Middle East (2015-2022)

According to God's end-time program, September 2015-2022 will be a season of war. Presently, Iran is seeking to develop nuclear weapons. This portends danger because it might lead to the proliferation of nuclear arms in the most volatile region of the world. That is why Israel, America, Germany, France, and the United Kingdom are looking for ways to prevent Iran from becoming a nuclear power. Unfortunately, all efforts to stop Iran from developing weapons of mass destruction will fail, and Israel will be in grave danger. The Russians will play a pivotal role in this game of chess in the Middle East. They will strengthen the Iranian Air Force and missile defense project and provide military, diplomatic, and moral support to Syria in order to checkmate the growing influence of the United States in the region.

Middle East Crisis

Many options have been placed on the table by the Israeli government to slow the Iranians from acquiring nuclear weapons.

Personal Insight: Attempts by the Israelis to destroy Iran's nuclear plant will not be completely successful. Hence, Iran will have weapons of mass destruction. Israel will be perceived as the aggressor in this crisis. Therefore

Israel will be isolated by many nations that have economic and religious ties to Arab nations. Arabs worldwide will be sympathetic to Iran. Hence Iran will be able to build alliance with many nations strong enough to threaten the survival of Israel. According to the prophet Ezekiel, Syria and Turkey will emerge to be Iran's allies in the Middle East.

A leader from Persia (Iran) in alliance with Syria will start a big war, although he will not be taken seriously in the beginning. Weapons of mass destruction will be used.

Middle East War

Personal Insight: What will begin as a regional conflagration will eventually involve the European Union, the United States, and Russia. This Middle East crisis will have a significant effect on the price of crude oil worldwide, although the West will be the hardest hit. In this war, the Arabs will systematically weaken the economy of the West. They will shut down the flow of oil to the Western world. This will cause the price of gasoline (and consequently the smooth running of governments in the West) to spiral out of control. The Arabs will do this because they want to punish the West for supporting Israel. The Chinese will get a greater supply of oil from the Middle East than Europe and the United States because they will ally with the Arabs. The Suez Canal and the Strait of Hormuz, the trade routes that enable the supply of oil from the Middle East to the Western world, will become significantly important. In order to keep the trade route open, the West will send a military reinforcement to protect the Suez Canal and the Strait of Hormuz.

The Suez Canal is strategically located to provide the shortest link between the Mediterranean and the Indian Ocean and has become the shipping lane for the passage of crude oil from the Middle East to Europe and United States. Because of its strategic importance, the canal has been the cause of major wars throughout history. For instance on July 26, 1956, it was nationalized by the Egyptian government. This move made Britain, France, and Israel very uncomfortable. For the Western powers, the Suez Canal is too strategic to be controlled by a single nation. War broke out in October 1956, with Britain, France, and Israel allied against Egypt. The Soviet Union supported Egypt and threatened to attack London, Paris, and Tel Aviv. In order to prevent the crisis from escalating into a global war, the United States pressured the Anglo-France-Israeli alliance into withdrawal from Egypt and encouraged the formation of a peacekeeping force under the administration of the United Nations to oversee the canal.

The Suez Canal was also instrumental in causing the Six-Day Warbetween Israel and Egypt, Transjordan, and Syria. In May 1967, the Egyptian president expelled the United Nations peacekeeping force from the canal and prevented Israel from using the straits of Tiran for shipping. This led to Israel's preemptive strike on Egypt in June 1967, precipitating a war that lasted six days.

Knowing how the Suez Canal has caused wars in the past helps us to appreciate the build up to the next war. At present, the international peacekeeping force in the Suez Canal region is known as the Multinational Force and Observers (MFO). Members of this force come from the European Union, the United States, Canada, and Australia. The headquarters of this force is in Rome. The MFO ensures freedom of international marine navigation in the Strait of Tiran and access to the Gulf of Aqaba.

The desire for peace on the part of both Egypt and Israel, combined with the effectiveness of the MFO, has resulted in a durable and lasting state of peace between these two nations. That is going to change soon. The Israeli-Egypt peace treaty will be violated.

The Western powers understand the threat that Iran poses to the entire world and are getting ready for war. They are also ready to protect the shipping lanes in the Middle East at all costs.

Personal Insight: War will break out between the Western troops protecting the canal and Arab troops trying to destroy it. There will be much confusion. Around the world, people will be calling for peace and dialogue to prevent the escalation of this conflict, but common sense will not prevail. Ego, pride, selfish ambition, and religious fundamentalist agendas will reign uncontrolled. NATO will have a leadership crisis: U.S. troops will disagree with British troops; new diplomatic and military alliances will emerge; the Russian leader will strategically ally with Syria and Iran to checkmate the growing influence of the U.S. in the Middle East. The U.S. will continue to use Israel as a proxy to maintain influence in the region. In spite of all attempts to resolve this serious regional conflict, full-scale war will be decreed. *An attempt by Iran and her allies to destroy Israel and the Suez canal/Strait of Hormuz will trigger the World War III.*

Invasion of the Middle East

The Russian army, with the speed of a well-prepared force, will invade the Middle East in order to fulfill the prophecy of Ezekiel given around 575 B.C. When the Russian army crosses into Lebanon, she has violated the Word; therefore she must be judged.

> . . . *You will come from your homeland in the distant north* with your vast cavalry and your mighty army, and you will attack my people Israel, covering their land like a cloud. At that time in the distant future, I will bring you against my land as everyone watches, and my holiness will be displayed by what happens to you, Gog. Then all the nations will know that I am the Lord. (Eze. 38:14-16, emphasis mine)

What powerful nation is directly located in the northern part of Israel? Russia.

Personal Insight: A very strong leader will soon emerge in Russia. This leader will be popular, charismatic, and egocentric. He will attempt to dominate the world. His influence will grow from Russia to the Middle East. This leader will form a very strong alliance with Iran and Syria and attempt to checkmate the influence of Western nations in the Middle East. By supporting the Arabs and blaming the U.S. and the European Union for the Middle East crisis, this leader will invade the entire Middle East in the name of peace, but his insidious intention will be to destroy Israel.

Russia Is Hooked

Prince Gog is the leader of a great army, the Russian army. Russia is located directly north of Israel. The biblical regions of Meshech and Tubal refer to Moscow and Tobolsk, which are located in Russia. According to Ezekiel, a leader is going to arise who is going to invade Israel for economic reasons. Which countries are going to be in league with the Russian army during this important invasion?

> *Persia, Ethiopia, and Libya* are with them, all of them with shield and helmet; *Gomer* and all its troops; the house of *Togarmah* from the far north and all its troops—many people are with you. (Eze. 38:5-6, emphasis mine)

The first country to be mentioned is Persia. This refers to modern-day Iran. In fact, Persia changed her name to Iran officially on March 21, 1935. Also listed are Libya, a North African Arab country, and Ethiopia. These will be supported directly or indirectly by Tunisia, Sudan, Morocco, Algeria, and Egypt. Then we have Gomer and Beth-togarmah, which refer to modern-day Turkey. This Russian-Arab alliance would not be complete without mentioning Syria and Lebanon. Their purpose?—To wipe Israel off the face of the Earth.

Some nations will be taken aback by the aggression of the Russian-Arab invasion of Israel. They will query the motive of the aggression and resist the invasion:

> "Sheba, Dedan, the merchants of Tarshish, and all their young lions will say to you, 'Have you come to take plunder? Have you gathered your army to take booty, to carry away silver and gold, to take away livestock and goods, to take great plunder?'" (Eze. 38:13)

Sheba and Dedan refer to people living in the Arabian Peninsula, which includes the modern-day nations of Saudi Arabia, Kuwait, and the United Arab Emirates. Tarshish was a city once located in what is now modern-day Spain, which is to the west of Israel. The "merchants of Tarshish" refer to the economic community of the Western world—the European Union, the United States, and Canada. "Young lions" refer to their political leaders. This passage shows that Saudi Arabia, Kuwait, and the United Arab Emirates will continue to be pro-West. For purely economic reasons, they will join the Israel-NATO alliance to fight against Russia. More importantly, Spain will play a critical role in checkmating the invasion of Europe by Russia.

Mountains of Israel

Where is the main battle going to take place? Let's look at what the prophet Ezekiel said:

> "And I will turn you around and lead you on, bringing you up from the far north, and bring you against the mountains of Israel." (Eze. 39:2)

The mountains of Israel are located in the northern part of the country. This refers to the Golan Heights. This strategically placed plateau and mountainous region is in close proximity to Syria. It extends from Lebanon, through Syria to the northern part of Jordan. During the 1967 war with Syria, Israel took over this mountainous range. At present, Israel governs, occupies, and controls two-third of the Golan Heights. In spite of intense international pressure to hand over this mountain to Syria, Israel is still holding onto it. In fact, many Arab leaders have averred that there will be no peace with Israel until the country reverts back to the pre-1967 border. This implies giving back the Golan Heights to Syria and the Temple Mount to Jordan. Israeli-NATO forces will stop the Russian-Arab invasion of Israel at the strategic Golan Heights. This war will be fierce at the northern border of Israel:

Ezekiel 38: 18-23, proclaims that a terrible weapon of destruction will be used in this war. Israel will be fighting for survival. Although she will be overwhelmed by the sheer number of enemies, she will fight like David fought in the days of old. When it appears that she is about to be defeated—when Israel can no longer withstand the power of her opponents, and politicians from the U.S. and Europe are putting pressure on NATO to stop intervening in what can be said to be a regional war—something phenomenal will happen. God will intervene. A great earthquake will occur, the magnitude and scale of destruction of which will be so great that it will strike terror into the hearts of the invading army. According to Ezekiel, mountains will be thrown down, cliffs will crumble, walls will fall, and confusion will come upon the invading army. This divine intervention will be a turning event in this cataclysmic war. The Russian-Arab forces will be routed by Israel and her allies. It will be apparent to everyone that Israel won the war through the power of God. This great earthquake will not only deliver Israel from her enemies but also bring about a spiritual rebirth.

This awesome display of God on behalf of the Jewish nation will bring about a great national revival. In that day, many people in Israel shall turn to the living God and to Jesus Christ. (Eze. 38:23, 39:22)

Russian-Iranian Alliance Defeated

According to Ezekiel 39: 1-7, five out of six parts of the invading army, will be destroyed. In other words, the invading army will be routed.

Personal Insight: Russian armies in the Middle East will be completely isolated and their supply cut off. They will be destroyed by the armies of Europe and North America. Weapons of mass destruction will be freely used, and it will be like a rain of death on the bewildered Russian soldiers. The force of the blast will destroy the Russian tanks and equipment of war like toys, and the unbearable heat will burn their flesh. The intense flashes of lightning from advanced weapons will blind many of the soldiers, who will wander around in the desert, only to die from wound infection, burns, and the blazing heat of the sun. *Palestine will be destroyed* during this war. Many oil fields will be set ablaze. Advanced secret weapons will be on display. *Syria will be soundly defeated.*

The weapons of war collected from the enemy will be used by Israel to generate energy for seven years. (Eze. 39:8-10)

This great deliverance will be followed by great revival among the Jewish people. (Eze. 39:28-29; Joel 2:20, 28-29)

Chapter Seven

Fourth Seal Part II: World War III
(September 2015-2022)

Fourth Event: War	Fourth Seal: War
"For nation will rise against nation, and kingdom against kingdom . . . All these are the beginning of sorrows." (Matt. 24:7,8, emphasis mine)	When he opened the fourth seal, I heard the voice of the fourth living creature saying, "Come and see." So I looked, and behold, a pale horse. And the name of him who sat on it was Death, and Hades followed with him. *And power was given to them over a fourth of the earth, to kill with sword, with hunger, with death, and by the beasts of the earth.* (Rev. 6:7-8, emphasis mine)

Between the years 2015 and 2022 A.D., this war described by the prophet Ezekiel in Ezekiel 38 and 39 may come upon the earth. It will be a great Middle East War that will spread and consume many other nations. Russia, the European Union, and the United States will be forced to participate, and this war will eventually become World War III. Though the Russian army and her allies will be defeated by divine intervention on the mountainous range of the Golan Heights, all Christians throughout the world should pay attention to what will be taking place in Turkey.

This chapter contains what I believe to be the most likely scenarios regarding World War III, the sign that the war has started, its progress, and how it will end. Moreover, we will appreciate the relationship between the war and the waves of tribulation that the people of God will face.

Tribulation Is Coming!

> And to the angel of the church in Smyrna write, ". . . Indeed, the devil is about to throw some of you into prison, that you may be tested, and *you will have tribulation ten days*. Be faithful until death, and I will give you the crown of life." (Rev. 2:8-10, emphasis mine)

Jesus said the church in Smyrna will have *tribulation for ten days*. He was not making reference to ten ordinary days but ten years—the biblical principle of a day for a year. A good illustration of this "day for a year" principle in God's prophetic calendar can be found in Daniel 9:24.

Seven weeks of 70 weeks translates to 70×7 days = 490 days. It is nearly universally accepted among biblical scholars that this was not a reference to 490 days but to 490 *years*, or the biblical "day for a year" principle. Furthermore, in Daniel 9:27, the prophet was talking about a covenant for one week, which equals seven days.

Again, bible scholars agree that this was a reference to seven years rather than seven days, and it is a peace that will soon be signed by Israel. So the concept of a day for a year is not strange to many students of biblical prophecies. The prophetic message that the church in Smyrna will have tribulation for ten days means the church will go through *ten turbulent years of fierce persecution*. The reference here can be both an actual number to the church in Smyrna specifically and at the same time symbolic to the end-time church.

Personal Insight: This perilous ten-year period will be characterized by schism in the church, world war, human microchip implant, and another attempt to exterminate the Jews.

However, the Holy Spirit wants us to understand the implication of the persecution of the church in Smyrna. Smyrna is an ancient city in modern-day Turkey. Today, the city is known as Izmir and is strategically located on the coast of the Aegean Sea. Since Turkey is a member of NATO, a United States Air Force Base, the 425th Air Base Squadron, is located in Izmir. Since the Aegean Sea opens into the Mediterranean, this base will be strategically significant during the coming Russian invasion of the Middle East. Having already met with defeat, the Russian Armed Forces will invade Turkey. Izmir will be destroyed. Smyrna represents Turkey, which will be invaded by the Russian army before the invasion of Europe. Hence the beginning of the ten-year tribulation period for Christians in many parts of the world will be marked by the invasion and destruction of Izmir.

Personal Insight: Turkey will be invaded by the Russian army before the invasion of the rest of Europe. This should be a sign to the Christians in Europe: When you see Turkey being invaded by the Russian-led military forces, move out of Europe because the World War III will be short, swift, and destructive. No single nation in Europe will be unaffected. The East and West coasts of the United States also will be in grave danger.

From Turkey, the war will spread to Italy, France, Spain, Germany, and the United Kingdom, the Christian nations in Europe. Many Christians will be caught in the crossfire. The aftermath of the World War III will be an attempt to establish a form of world government, a form of world currency, and a form of world religion, and this will lead to the global persecution of the faithful followers of Christ. Simultaneously, the power of the Holy Spirit will come mightily upon the men and women of God worldwide to take the gospel of the kingdom to the ends of the earth. What a mystery! The greatest persecution of the people of God will coincide with the greatest move of the Holy Spirit.

This is why the Holy Spirit is putting this book in your hands. We need to be prepared for the fiery tribulation that is coming. This is the time to press forward with the gospel of the kingdom because masses of souls are waiting to be swept into the kingdom of God. This is not the time to be fearful, but a time to be bold in the Holy Spirit, knowing that the Lord is in control and that He is with us until the end of the age.

During the ten years of severe persecution of Christians, the great commission Jesus gave to the church will be accomplished in the power of the Holy Spirit. The gospel of the kingdom will be taken to the ends of the earth.

Europe: The Great Battlefield

Europe is going to pay for the defeat of the Russians in the Middle East. NATO will be blamed. When you see Turkey being invaded, know that the World War III has begun.

Personal Insight: War will break out in Europe in the spring of April or May between 2015 and 2022 A.D. Like a well-oiled machine, the Russian army will invade many European countries. Yugoslavia, Austria, Hungary, and Italy will fall and be occupied. France will be in turmoil; the southern part of France will support the enemy. The Russians will attack Spain and attempt to capture Gibraltar, but will be delayed and eventually stopped at Spain's mountainous Pyrenees.

While invading the southern region of Europe, the Russians will simultaneously invade Europe from the north in an attempt to capture Germany and encircle Europe. Initially, the Russians will gain the upper hand against Germany. Russia's focus will be to capture Germany's industrial cities and destroy them. Germany will fiercely resist the invading army. Nuclear weapons will be freely used. *The United States Army will fight side by side with the German Army.* Russia's communication system will be attacked and destroyed. An invisible nuclear wall will be set up in Germany, and whoever passes through will be destroyed. Many Russian military tanks will unknowingly pass through this invisible wall and be destroyed. A great German leader will emerge during this war and take control of the German Army. Overnight, the tide of the battle will shift and the Russians will begin to lose.

At the mountainous Pyrenees, German, American, and Spanish soldiers will press against the Russian military and defeat them. When the Russians are stopped at Gibraltar, they will begin to use ballistic missiles with nuclear warheads against Europe. The southern part of England will be in grave danger.

Within four months of the invasion of Europe, when Russia's defeat seems imminent, some cities on the Eastern and Western coasts of the United States will be in grave danger. The Pentagon, White House, and a number of military installations will be targeted by the Russians, but the United States will counterattack with superior nuclear power. Cities in Russia will burn. Total defeat of the Russian army is decreed. The defeat of Russia will trigger a revolution, which if not well handled may lead to civil war in Russia. This revolution will sweep away the leaders who attacked Israel, and new ones will emerge. These new leaders will promise to cooperate with the Western world to rebuild Russia and prevent another nuclear holocaust. In the future, Russia will be a strategic ally of the Western nations.

According to the prophet Joel, the enemy from the north will be driven back from the Western nations to the East in shame. (Joel 2:20)

Rome Will Be Destroyed

Rome, the capital of Italy and the country's largest and most populated city is located on seven hills. The seven hills are:

- Aventine Hill
- Caelian Hill

- Capitoline Hill
- Esquiline Hill
- Palatine Hill
- Quirinal Hill
- Viminal Hill

According to Revelation, this city set on seven hills will be burned.

> "Here is the mind which has wisdom: *The seven heads are seven mountains on which the woman sits* . . . . And the ten horns which you saw on the beast, these will hate the harlot, make her desolate and naked, eat her flesh and *burn her with fire* . . . . And the woman whom you saw is that great city which reigns over the kings of the earth." (Rev. 17:9, 16, 18, emphasis mine)

During the invasion of Europe, Italy will be attacked. However, the superpowers in the European Union will delay in helping. Why? Its political leaders in Europe will have become fed up with the overbearing attitude of some religious leaders. Many will drift away from God towards secular humanism and technology. Many will believe that religion is the root cause of the Middle East crisis and therefore the problem of the world. When Rome is attacked and Vatican City is under siege, the European superpowers will be slow in engaging the invading enemy. Vatican City will be destroyed and the Pope's life will be in danger.

Personal Insight: The destruction of Vatican City will be preceded by a schism in the church. This great division will start from the largest denominational church in the world.

Schism in the Church: 2015-2022 A.D.

Personal Insight: Just as the land of Israel will be divided in the nearest future, the church of God will be divided. A pope will be elected that will bring disharmony to the Christian church. This future pope will cause division among bishops, cardinals, priests, and members of the Roman Catholic Church. This is the pope who will promote ecumenism and interreligious dialogue. This leader will attempt to move the Christian church in the direction of one-world religion because he desires to be its leader. Some denominational leaders in conjunction with renowned theologians will espouse the idea that Christians, Muslims, and Jews have one common denominator, worshipping the same God. The only theological precept dividing adherents of the three religions is Christ. Therefore, Christ will be relegated to the background. This is a *pseudo*-Christian church, not the one redeemed by Jesus Christ. How can there be a Christian church without Jesus Christ as the worthy Lamb of God that took away the sins of the world?

This strange religion will come out of Vatican City. In the name of peace, many Christians will be tempted to participate. Methodist, Episcopal, Baptist, Pentecostal, charismatic, and many other denominations will be invited to join in the conference for world religion in the name of peace. Be warned! This world religion is not from God but the fulfillment of the falling away from the faith:

> . . . Let no one deceive you by any means; for that Day will not come unless the falling away comes first, and the man of sin is revealed, the son of perdition. (2 Thess. 2:1-3)

Personal Insight: Between 2015 and 2022 A.D., the largest denominational church in the world will be rocked and shaken. There will be a split. One side will go with the new world religion espoused and headed by the future pope. The other will stand faithful to the Word of God and the testimony of Jesus Christ. At this time, the worldly church and some political leaders will use the power of the state to persecute the faithful church. This is in fulfillment of the Word of God:

> So he carried me away in the Spirit into the wilderness. And I saw a woman sitting on a scarlet beast which was full of names of blasphemy,

having seven heads and ten horns. The woman was arrayed in purple and scarlet, and adorned with gold and precious stones and pearls, having in her hand a golden cup full of abominations and the filthiness of her fornication. And on her forehead a name was written: MYSTERY, BABYLON THE GREAT, THE MOTHER OF HARLOTS AND OF THE ABOMINATIONS OF THE EARTH. I saw the woman, drunk with the blood of the saints and with the blood of the martyrs of Jesus. And when I saw her, I marveled with great amazement. (Rev. 17: 3-6)

France Will Be Weakened

Personal Insight: France will be damaged but not destroyed during the invasion of Europe by the Russians. The southern part of France will support the invading army. Some cities will be burned down.

England Will Fall

Personal Insight: The southern part of England will be severely affected.

Judgment of Three Nations

The influence, power, and glory of three powerful nations in Europe will be greatly curtailed during this war. The prophet Daniel saw a vision of what will happen at this time:

After this I saw in the night visions, and behold, a fourth beast, dreadful and terrible, exceedingly strong . . . and it had ten horns. I was considering the horns, and there was another horn, a little one, coming up among them, before whom three of the first horns were plucked out by the roots.

And there, in this horn, were eyes like the eyes of a man, and a mouth speaking pompous words. (Dan. 7:7-8)

This vision is related to what will happen between 2015 and 2022 A.D. The fourth beast refers to the European Union, with its ten permanent members. These ten are members of both NATO and the European Union. They are the only nations that have full voting rights:

- United Kingdom
- France
- Germany
- Italy
- Belgium

- Netherlands
- Luxembourg
- Portugal
- Spain
- Greece

According to Daniel 7:8, a new leader will emerge on the world scene that will cause the global influence of three of the above ten nations to be diminished. The little horn, the new leader, will replace the three nations in influence, glory, and power.

The three nations to fall are the United Kingdom, France, and Italy because they occupied the land of Israel between 70 and 1948 A.D. *These are the three horns to be uprooted from the European Union.*

History of Jerusalem between 70 and 1948 A.D.

A summary of the history of the occupation of the land of Israel between 70 and 1948 A.D. shows that Italy, France, Turkey, and the United Kingdom had not only occupied the land but at times killed and prevented the Jews from coming back to Jerusalem. The list below shows the nations and empires that took control of Jerusalem during this time.

1. Roman Empire: 70-638 A.D.
2. Muslim Arab (Jihadists): 638-1099 A.D.; the Dome of the Rock was built 685-691 A.D.

3. Christian crusaders, mostly from France; 1099-1187 A.D. They killed Jews and Muslims. Jerusalem became the capital city of the Christian kingdom.
4. Muslim Arabs recaptured Jerusalem 1187-1517 A.D.
5. The Ottoman Turks took control of Jerusalem between 1517 and 1917 A.D. (the Ottoman Empire remains today as modern-day Turkey)
6. The British Empire took control of Jerusalem 1917-1948 A.D. (just after World War I).
7. In 1922, the British Empire gave 80 percent of the original Jewish land to Transjordan (modern-day Jordan) in order to appease the Arabs.
8. In 1939 the British Empire restricted Jewish immigration into Jerusalem to appease the Arabs.
9. In 1945 the British Empire prevented many Jews running away from the Holocaust from entering Jerusalem in order to appease the Arabs. In 1947, the British Empire submitted the remaining Jewish land to the United Nations for administration. In May 17, 1948, an independent Jewish state was established by the power of Jehovah Elohim.

Because of their occupation of Jerusalem 70-1948 A.D., the judgment of God is coming upon the United Kingdom, France, and Italy. For the same reason, Turkey will be judged and the Dome of the Rock will be destroyed.

Chapter Eight

The Little Horn, the Beast, and the False Prophet (September 2015-2022)

There will be three influential world leaders who will attempt to dominate the global political landscape between 2015 and 2022. The first one is labeled "the little horn," the second is "the beast", and the third will be known as "the false prophet." In this chapter, we will discuss the emergence of these three leaders, the prophetic messages regarding them, and the nature of the new world order they will try to create.

Emergence of the Little Horn

The prophet Daniel gave a very detailed description of who the little horn is and from where he will arise. Let us pay attention to the Word of God:

> Then I lifted my eyes and saw, and there, standing beside the river, was a ram which had two horns, and the two horns were high; but one was higher than the other, and the higher one came up last. I saw the ram pushing westward, northward, and southward, so that no animal could withstand him; nor was there any that could deliver from his hand, but he did according to his will and became great. (Dan. 8:3-4)

The ram in this vision is a reference to the Great Medo-Persian Empire that rose up after the Babylonian

Empire. As prophesied, eventually the Persians became greater than the Medes.

> And as I was considering, suddenly a male goat came from the west, across the surface of the whole earth, without touching the ground; and the goat had a notable horn between his eyes. Then he came to the ram that had two horns, which I had seen standing beside the river, and ran at him with furious power. And I saw him confronting the ram; he was moved with rage against him, attacked the ram, and broke his two horns. There was no power in the ram to withstand him, but he cast him down to the ground and trampled him; and there was no one that could deliver the ram from his hand. Therefore the male goat grew very great; but when he became strong, the large horn was broken, and in place of it four notable ones came up toward the four winds of heaven. (Dan. 8:5-8)

The male goat in this vision refers to the growth of the Greek Empire, which is represented by Alexander the Great, who came from Macedonia in the west to conquer the Medo-Persian Empire. After the death of Alexander the Great, the empire was divided into four parts, fulfilling the vision given to Daniel. The four kingdoms that came out of the Grecian Empire are known today as Greece, Turkey, Syria, and Egypt:

> And out of one of them came *a little horn* which grew exceedingly great toward *the south, toward the east, and toward the Glorious Land.* And it grew up to the host of heaven; and it cast down some of the host and some of the stars to the ground, and trampled them. He even exalted himself as high as the prince of the host; and *by him the daily sacrifices were taken away,* and the place of the sanctuary was cast down. Because of transgression, an army was given over to the horn to oppose the daily sacrifices; and he cast truth

down to the ground. He did all this and prospered. (Dan. 8:9-12, emphasis mine)

Out of one of these four kingdoms, a leader shall arise whose influence will grow to the *southern* part of Israel (that is, Egypt, Libya, Sudan, Algeria, Somalia, Morocco, Tunisia, and Yemen) to the *eastern* part of Israel (that is, Jordan, Saudi Arabia, Iraq, Iran, and Kuwait) and toward the Glorious Land (that is, Israel, Syria, Lebanon, and Palestine). This is the man who will set up the abomination that makes desolate by forcefully putting an end to daily sacrifices in the temple. This man will bring transgression to full measure, cast truth to the ground, and prosper. He shall be one of the richest men on earth.

Personal Insight: After the influence of Italy, France, and the United Kingdom has been whittled, this man (the little horn) will arise to create an economic partnership between the European Union and the Arab countries. He will be a candidate for the Nobel Prize for peace.

According to the apostle Paul, this man will take control of the third temple to be built in the future and proclaim himself to be God. (2 Thess. 2:3-4)

This man will be an Arab leader. The prophet Isaiah called him "the Assyrian":

> Therefore thus says the Lord God of hosts: "O my people, who dwell in Zion, do not be afraid of the Assyrian. He shall strike you with a rod and lift up his staff against you, in the manner of Egypt." (Isa. 10:24)

There will be a resurrection of the Assyrian Empire. Syria, Jordan, Iran, Iraq, Lebanon, Palestine, Turkey, the northern kingdom of Israel, and Egypt were under the rule of the ancient Assyrian Empire around 720 B.C. Four hundred years later, all of these countries came under the rule of the Greek Empire around 320 B.C. Therefore, both the prophets Daniel and Isaiah were referring to the same geographic region that will produce the man of lawlessness. The prophet Isaiah referred to him as an Assyrian; Daniel saw him rise from one of the four kingdoms derived from the Grecian Empire. Therefore, when we see the nation of Turkey becoming a regional power in the Middle East, we know that the Assyrian Empire has been resurrected.

Personal Insight: Turkey is going to be a regional power in the Middle East. Just like the European Union, countries will come together in the Middle East to have a common currency and a loose federation. After the fall of the current U.S. dollar, this union of Arab countries will have a very significant impact on the emerging world currency. Moreover, this union of Arab nations will produce a great leader, someone who is very diplomatic, crafty, and deceptive, and one who appears peaceful but is very wicked. He will be very friendly with many Western leaders, and in the name of peace he will destroy many. This leader from a small country in the Middle East is the little horn.

The Beast with Seven Heads

> The beast that you saw was, and is not, and will ascend out of the bottomless pit and go to perdition. And those who dwell on the earth will marvel, whose names are not written in the Book of Life from the foundation of the world, when they see the beast that was, and is not, and yet is. (Rev. 17:8)

This beast is not an ordinary human being, but the devil incarnate. Just as Jesus Christ is the son of God, this man is the son of the devil, Satan, the enemy of our souls. (Rev. 13:2)

This man is going to come in the power and glory of principalities and powers. According to Revelation 13:8, "All who dwell on the earth will worship him, whose names have not been written in the Book of Life of the Lamb slain from the foundation of the world." The whole world will wonder at his wisdom, oratory prowess, political skill, administrative ability, and decisiveness. This man will resurrect Hitler's political and philosophical ideology of dominating the world.

Seven Heads = Seven Kings

> "Here is the mind which has wisdom: The seven heads are seven mountains on which the woman sits. There are also *seven kings. Five have fallen, one is, and the other has not yet come. And when he comes, he must continue a short time."* (Rev. 17:9-10, emphasis mine)

These seven kings are seven human agents, kings and rulers, used by the devil throughout history to attempt to destroy the plan of God's salvation for mankind, by attempting to destroy children of Israel. Let us look at each of the seven in turn:

1. Amenhotep I, king of Egypt (1546-1526 B.C.)

This was the first king who attempted to annihilate the children of Israel in the Scriptures. This King instructed Hebrew midwives to kill male children of Hebrew women during childbirth but allow the female ones to live. However, the midwives feared God and allowed the male children to live. Hence, God blessed the midwives. (Ex. 1:15-20)

2. Sennacherib, king of Assyria (704-681 B.C.)

In 721 B.C., the Assyrians, under the kingship of Shalmaneser V, destroyed Israel's northern kingdom and threatened the existence of her southern kingdom. However, twenty years later, in 701 B.C., Sennacherib, king of Assyria, attacked the southern kingdom during the reign of King Hezekiah and took all the fenced cities of Judah.

Jerusalem was the last city to be defeated. When all hope was lost, King Hezekiah and the prophet Isaiah prayed to the Lord. God answered and delivered them. (2 Kings 19:32-36)

3. Nebuchadnezzar, king of Babylon (605-562 B.C.)

This was the king who eventually destroyed Israel's southern kingdom and carried the people to Babylon in 586 B.C. (2 Kings 25:21)

However, by divine intervention, Israel was restored back to the southern part of Israel. (Ezra 1:1-3)

4. Ahasuerus (Xerxes I), king of Persia (485-465 B.C.)

King Ahasuerus was the husband of Queen Esther in the Scriptures. This king was deceived by one of the highly placed officials in his kingdom, Haman, who hated the Jews and misrepresented them before the king. Hence, the king gave the order that all Jews in his kingdom should be destroyed (Esther 3:8-11).

The living God enabled Esther, the queen, to find favor before the king and represented the Jews until the law written for their destruction was counteracted. (Esther 8:10-12)

That great deliverance is still remembered and celebrated by the Jews today. This is known as Purim, a festival celebrated annually according to the Hebrew calendar on the fourteenth day of the Hebrew month of Adar.

5. Antiochus IV Epiphanes: ruler of the Seleucid Empire (Syria) (175-164 B.C.)

This was this king who came against Jerusalem and took it. He killed more than thirty thousand Jews. He was a *type* of the man of lawlessness who is coming. Antiochus Epiphanes was the first man in the history of the Jews who desecrated the temple and the altar of the living God. He did an abominable thing by offering swine flesh upon the altar thereby desecrating the temple. This event is known as an "abomination that made desolate." He successfully and forcefully put an end to the daily sacrifices; the temple became desolate. He also broke into the most holy section of the temple and cast away the golden vessels and other precious sacred items.

Moreover, in a very bold disregard for God, Antiochus prohibited Jewish worship and dedicated the temple to an Athenian god, Jupiter Olympus. He attempted to destroy Jewish worship of the living God. However, under the leadership of the Maccabees, a remnant of Jews revolted and fought against Antiochus. God gave victory to the Jews, and true temple worship was restored.

That great deliverance is still being remembered and celebrated by the Jews worldwide today. This feast is known as the festival of lights, Hanukkah. This is a commemoration of the restoration of the Jerusalem temple after its desecration. The feast is observed for eight nights and usually takes place in November/December.

6. Roman Emperor Titus (79-81 A.D.)

Before he became an emperor, Titus was the Roman military commander responsible for the destruction of Jerusalem and the temple in 70 A.D. Eventually, Jews were scattered from their land. This emperor dealt a devastating blow to the Jews. To this day, the temple has not been rebuilt.

The book of Revelation was written by the apostle John while he was banished to Patmos Island during the reign of Emperor Titus. At that time, the above named five kings had fallen, but the sixth king, Titus, was still in reign.

Therefore the Scriptures proclaim that five kings had fallen, one is and one is yet to come:

> "There are also seven kings. Five have fallen, one is, and the other has not yet come. And when he comes, he must continue a short time." (Rev. 17:10)

7. Adolf Hitler of Germany (1933-1945)

This was the latest figure in history who has sought to destroy the Jews from the earth. He was the leader of Nazi Germany who brought about the systematic extermination of about *six million Jews* during World War II, a period known as the Holocaust. His end came suddenly in April 1945.

> *"The beast that was, and is not, is himself also the eighth, and is of the seven, and is going to perdition.* The ten horns which you saw are ten kings who have received no kingdom as yet, but they receive authority for one hour as kings with the beast." (Rev. 17:11-12)

8. The beast

According to the above Scripture, this man is coming in our immediate future. He is of the seventh king. Since the seventh king, Adolf Hitler, was from Germany, the future king will also come from Germany and will be a leader of the European Union with the ten permanent members: Italy, Germany, France, the United Kingdom, Spain, the Netherlands, Greece, Belgium, Portugal, and Luxembourg.

German Leader: The Beast and the War Hero

Personal Insight: The World War III, which will occur with the invasion of Europe by the Russians, will be very short but destructive. It will start in the spring, April or May, of the chosen year. Within two months, nations will be destroyed. Russian soldiers will run through southern Europe in an attempt to capture Gibraltar, but will encounter a problem with Spain. Also Russia's thrust from the north through Germany will be met with great force and an invisible nuclear wall. The Russian army will be defeated. With the fall of Italy, France, and the United Kingdom, Germany will be the most powerful nation in Europe. By September/October of the same year, a German leader will declare victory in Europe, and many people will rejoice.

This German leader will be a great war hero. Many people will say, "Who is like this war hero and who can fight against him?" This is to fulfill the Word of God in Revelation 13:4: "So they worshiped the dragon who gave authority to the beast; and they worshiped the beast, saying, 'Who is like the beast? *Who is able to make war with him?'* This leader will begin to dominate the political landscape of Germany between 2015 and 2022 A.D. He will be charismatic, shrewd, ambitious, experienced, and well connected. This is the man who will attempt to exercise political control over the whole world. *This is the man referred to as the beast in the Scripture.*

The *beast,* a very ambitious politician from Germany, will attempt to finish the work that the seven previous agents attempted: total annihilation of the Jews. To do this, the beast (a European leader) will form an alliance with the little horn (an Arab leader) to fulfill the prophecy of Daniel:

> The fourth beast shall be a fourth kingdom on earth, which shall be different from all other kingdoms, and shall devour the whole earth, trample it and break it in pieces. The ten horns are ten kings who shall arise from this kingdom. And another shall rise after them; he shall be different from the first ones, and shall subdue three kings. He shall speak pompous words against the Most High, shall persecute the saints of the Most High,

and shall intend to change times and law. Then the saints shall be given into his hand for a time and times and half a time. (Dan. 7:23-25)

This vision given to Daniel is very loaded. It will be very helpful to take note of the details given here.

1. The beast shall be a political leader of the emerging new world order. He will be a German leader who is ready to do abominable things, including annihilate the Jews in order to dominate the world. (Dan. 7:23)
2. The ten permanent members of the European Union will be the foundation of this new world order. (Dan. 7:24a)
3. Another regional leader shall arise after the formation of the European Union. This is the little horn of Scripture, called "the Assyrian" by the prophet Isaiah. This leader will ally with the European Union in forming the new world order. (Dan. 7:24b)
4. This Arab leader (the little horn/Assyrian) shall be different from the European leaders in color, language, religion, and worldview. (Dan. 7:24b)
5. This Arab leader shall amass great political and military strength by maintaining a delicate balance of relationships between the European Union, the United States, Russia, China, and the Arab world. (Personal Insight)
6. This little horn, the Arab leader, shall persecute the Jews and Christians by secretly organizing, promoting, and spreading Jihad. (Dan. 7:25a)
7. This little horn/the Assyrian will push for constitutional changes in the Arab countries. These are changes that will produce economic, political, and military cooperation among the Arab countries. (Dan. 7:25b)
8. The beast, the little horn, and all their allies will reign as leaders of the new world order for three-and-one-half years. (Dan. 7:25b)

Behold, Another Beast!

> Then I saw *another beast* coming up out of the earth, and he had *two horns like* a lamb and spoke like a dragon. And he exercises all the authority of the first beast in his presence, and causes the earth and those who dwell in it to worship the first beast, whose deadly wound was healed. He performs great signs, so that *he even makes fire come down from heaven* on the earth in the sight of men. And he deceives those who dwell on the earth by those signs which he was granted to do in the sight of the beast, telling those who dwell on the earth to make an image to the beast who was wounded by the sword and lived. *He was granted power to give breath to the image of the beast*, that the image of the beast should both speak and cause as many as would not worship the image of the beast to be killed. *He causes all, both small and great, rich and poor, free and slave, to receive a mark on their right hand or on their foreheads*, and that no one may buy or sell except one who has the mark or the name of the beast, or the number of his name. Here is wisdom. Let him who has understanding calculate the number of the beast, for it is the number of a man: his number is 666. (Rev. 13: 11-18, emphasis mine)

In the nearest future, another beast will emerge who will head a powerful kingdom. This second beast will give life to the formation of the new world order. That is, this second beast will make the idea of a new world order become a reality.

1. This last beast represents the last global leader to be manifested during the lifespan of this generation.
2. The beast will have two horns, meaning that two kings or two countries will come together and give up their sovereignty to the beast. (Rev. 13:11)
3. Like a lamb, this kingdom will talk about peace, work for peace, and be the vanguard in peacekeeping

all over the world. Like a lamb, this kingdom will be founded on Judeo-Christian values. Like a lamb, this kingdom will work to establish the kingdom of God by human power and human wisdom.

4. "He makes fire to come down from heaven": This kingdom will be able to wage warfare from space. (Rev. 13:13)
5. "He was granted power to give breath to the image of the beast": This kingdom will have the power to bring the idea of new world order into reality. (Rev. 13:15)
6. This kingdom will argue that many societal benefits can be derived from the human implant of microchips. In the name of prosperity and security, the practice of microchip implant will be promoted by this kingdom. (Rev. 13:16)
7. This kingdom will exercise control over the world's economy and cause a global shift toward a cashless society. (Rev. 13:17)

Personal Insight: A leader of the alliance of the North American countries (the United States, Canada, and Mexico) will in the future become the false prophet (Rev. 13:1-18), who in the name of safety and security turns the whole region into a police state.

New World Order: 2018-2029 A.D.

The new world order will emerge between 2018 and 2029 A.D. It will be characterized by global currency, global governance, and world religion. A leader will arise in Germany who will be the war hero of the World War III. This leader will exercise great political power throughout the whole world. Moreover, he will be supported by the leader of the North Americas, who in the name of transatlantic economic development will combine the economies of Europe with those of North America, creating a super-economy able to dominate the world. In the name of security, the new world order will promote a cashless society through innovation and creativity that will give birth to microchips being implanted in the right hands and foreheads of human beings in many countries. When this happens, this will be a fulfillment of the Word of God:

> He causes all, both small and great, rich and poor, free and slave, to receive a mark on their right hand or on their foreheads, and that no one may buy or sell except one who has the mark or the name of the beast, or the number of his name. (Rev. 13:16-17)

Personal Insight: This is written for the patience and endurance of the saints. Between 2018 and 2029 A.D., money in form of microchips and global currency will begin to manifest. Around this time, a form of world religion that is inclusive (because Jesus Christ has been taken out of the equation) will begin to spread. People of God, we need to watch out lest we are deceived by the enemy. There will be a new world order characterized by one world currency, global governance, and a form of world religion. To receive a microchip on the right hand or forehead is to receive the mark of the beast and become a member of this emerging world order. The wrath of God is coming upon everyone who receives the microchip.

> Then a third angel followed them, saying with a loud voice, "If anyone worships the beast and his image, *and receives his mark on his forehead or on his hand, he himself shall also drink of the wine of the wrath of God, which is poured out full strength into the cup of his indignation* . . . Then I heard a voice from heaven saying to me, *"Write: 'Blessed are the dead who die in the Lord from now on.'"* "Yes," says the Spirit, *"that they may rest from their labors, and their works follow them."* (Rev. 14:9-13, emphasis mine)

Many children of God will resist the forces of new world order to the end. They will refuse to take the microchips. Some will be tortured while others will be killed, but the Spirit of the living God says to them, "Blessed are the dead who die in the Lord from now on." "Yes," says the Spirit, "that they may rest from their labors, and their works follow them." (Rev. 14:13)

It is much better to forsake the world with its lusts and temptations and gain eternal life in Christ Jesus.

Microchip Human Implant: The Mark of the Beast

Personal Insight: It shall come to pass that a man of great influence shall arise, who will achieve an extraordinary breakthrough in the field of DNA computer microchips. This man will become very rich from this feat. He will be a philanthropist with many humanitarian programs. He will be an activist who will appeal to the spirit of ecumenism to help many poor communities. He will come across as a savior to many people. This will be Satan appearing as angel of light. (2 Cor. 11:14)

Personal Insight: This Assyrian (the little horn) will attempt to control the world's economy by going into partnership with the advanced countries of this world. Great multinational corporations will be enriched by marketing his microchips. In the name of prosperity and security, nations will begin to accept this technology. The plan is to have people in the world mandated by law to receive this microchip into their right hands or foreheads. This man will gain power through economic control via computer technology.

This implant will be accomplished using laser technology and will be very fast, painless, and invisible. This microchip will contain all of the personal information of the individual carrying the chip—bank account, healthcare information, genetic makeup, and security codes for those working in restricted places. This chip will enable law enforcement agents to be more effective in their investigations and allow governments to exercise more control over their citizens. However, the chip will also be used to eliminate people labeled as burdens on society, such as those with terminal illnesses, the very old with chronic illnesses, and those who are severely handicapped. This system will be created to eradicate those who cannot contribute positively to the economic prosperity of the state. Indirectly, these people will be murdered by their own government in the name of prosperity. Those who refuse to have microchip implants will become social outcasts, unable to be gainfully employed in many places and will be denied government services.

Do not take this mark! It is evil. Its end is destruction. Maybe you are asking, "How am I going to eat and survive? What am I going to do? What about my family and children? How am I going to pay my bills?"

This is the Word of God to you:

> Therefore do not worry, saying, 'What shall we eat?' or 'What shall we drink?' or 'What shall we wear?' For after all these things the Gentiles seek. For your heavenly Father knows that you need all these things. But seek first the kingdom of God and his righteousness, and all these things shall be added to you. Therefore do not worry about tomorrow, for tomorrow will worry about its own things. Sufficient for the day is its own trouble. (Matt. 6:31-34)

Chapter Nine

Fifth Seal Part I: The Tribulation Period (September 2022-2029 A.D.)

Fifth Event: Great Persecution of the Followers of Christ	Fifth Seal: Great Persecution of the Followers of Christ
"Then they will deliver you up to tribulation and kill you, and you will be hated by all nations for my name's sake . . . But he who endures to the end shall be saved. And this gospel of the kingdom will be preached in all the world as a witness to all the nations, and then the end will come." (Matt 24: 9-14, emphasis mine)	When he opened the fifth seal, *I saw under the altar the souls of those who had been slain for the word of God and for the testimony which they held.* And they cried with a loud voice, saying, "How long, O Lord, holy and true, until You judge and avenge our blood on those who dwell on the earth?" (Rev. 6: 9-10, emphasis mine)
The Coming Great Jewish Holocaust	**The Coming Great Jewish Holocaust**
"Therefore when you see the 'abomination of desolation,' spoken of by Daniel the prophet, standing in the holy place" (whoever reads, let him understand), "then let those who are in Judea flee to the mountains . . . *For then there will be great tribulation, such as has not been since the beginning of the world until this time, no, nor ever shall be."* (Matt. 24:15-21, emphasis mine)	Then a white robe was given to each of them; and it was said to them that they should rest a little while longer, until both the number of their fellow servants and their brethren, who would be killed as they were, was completed. (Rev. 6:11, emphasis mine)

The Bible passages above declare that severe persecution is coming upon the followers of Jesus Christ in these last days. In addition, great tribulation is coming upon the Jews. This chapter focuses on the waves of tribulation that are coming upon the bride of Christ in order to purge, cleanse, and prepare her for the bridegroom, Jesus Christ, our Lord and Savior. As discussed above, this tribulation period will start with the World War III during the fourth seal, which spans from 2015-2022 A.D. Hence, at the opening of the fifth seal in 2022 A.D., some souls are already in heaven crying for divine judgment against the inhabitants of the earth:

> When he opened the fifth seal, *I saw under the altar the souls of those who had been slain for the word of God and for the testimony which they held.* And they cried with a loud voice, saying, "How long, O Lord, holy and true, until you judge and avenge our blood on those who dwell on the earth?" (Rev. 6:9-10, emphasis mine)

There will be major waves of tribulation within the next two decades.

First Wave of Tribulation: World War III

This wave of tribulation has been discussed extensively in previous chapters. With the growing influence of the North American countries and the European Union on the global stage, China and Russia will attempt to respond by creating an alternate power structure. The great move for world domination will occur when Russia, in the name of keeping peace, invades the Middle East. Eventually, Russia will join the enemies of the nation of Israel to change the status of an ongoing regional war to a world war. According to Ezekiel 38 and 39, Russia in alliance with many nations in the Middle East will be defeated at the Golan Heights by the Israel Defense Force supported by the NATO. The Lord will intervene on behalf of Israel and destroy the invading army from the north.

However, Russia will refuse to be humiliated in war and will press forward with her political agenda to rule the world. In a very bold and unpredictable move, Russia will invade Turkey, and before anyone realizes what is happening, Western Europe will be under attack. Rome will fall under heavy fire from the invading army. The Pope, the cardinals, the bishops, the priests, and many faithful men and women of God in Rome will be caught in the crossfire. Lives will be lost. A major Christian denomination will be under attack by the joint alliance of communism and extremists in the Islamic religion. The destruction of Vatican City will cause the whole world to mourn.

Major Christian nations in Europe will witness great destruction of their major cities. France, Germany, the United Kingdom, and Italy will be greatly affected. Many lives and properties will be lost in these nations, and many will become homeless. Eventually, the United States will join forces with the European army to defeat Russia. New advanced weapons, never before used in warfare, will be utilized to bring the war to a quick end.

This war will be brief but destructive. Starting in the spring of the chosen year (April/May), it will last about five months. By September of the same year, around the time of the feast of Yom Kippur, the whole world will be talking of peace. So this first wave of tribulation will last for only five months, and within this period millions of Christians in North Africa, the Middle East, Turkey, Russia, Italy, Germany, France, Greece, the United Kingdom, and the United States will be severely affected. In a single day, a whole country will lie in ruin. The wickedness of the heart of humanity will be revealed. Knowing that his time is short, the devil is bringing nations down in order to set up one world government, and in the process, Christians and their ministries are being attacked. This wave of tribulation will end with a seven-year peace treaty signed by all world leaders in September/October of the chosen year.

Second Wave of Tribulation: Global Currency

With terrorism on the rise and political instability of many states in the world, people will crave prosperity and security. The economy of the United States will be brought to its knees, and global economic gloom will be so prevalent that people will desire and receive with joy any perceived viable solution to their economic woes, even if it involves invasion of personal privacy and setting up a world currency. So shall it be—a world currency. The world is heading toward a global financial revolution.

This currency will come into being following the complete integration of the economies of the European Union with those of North America. The birth of this currency is likely to be midwived by the Transatlantic Economic Council (TEC), Transatlantic Business Dialogue (TABD), World Bank, International Monetary Fund, and political leaders from Europe and North America. Although it appears impossible today, this is the ultimate end of the present recurrent global economic crisis that will be witnessed within the next three years. TABD will continue to advocate for a barrier-free transatlantic market in order to promote economic growth and job creation in Europe and the United States. Canada and Mexico will be increasingly integrated into this major intercontinental economic cooperation.

Although there is nothing wrong with economic cooperation among countries and continents, men and women of God will understand spiritually that any world currency is a front designed by a few people to exercise unjust control over billions of people. Although it may sound good in theory, the problem of sin, greed, and selfishness cannot be curtailed by economic policies. This idea of integrating world-dominating economies to produce super economies could easily be hijacked by a few to exercise corrupt control over the resources of the world. As John Dalberg said in a letter in 1887, "Power tends to corrupt, and absolute power corrupts absolutely. Great men are almost always bad men." This will be the end result—the corruption of the political process and political leaders in Europe and North America and the emergence of a new form of slavery.

From the appearance of the first concrete steps toward bringing a world currency into existence, men and women of God worldwide will protest. Resistance movements will be formed in many nations to prevent their governments from participating, but such movements will find that they are doing too little too late. There will be a global currency.

Although small in numbers, resistance movements will be so vigorous in their protests against the perceived system of control that many of their leaders will be jailed and some killed, but "the people who know their God will be strong and do exploits" (Dan. 11:32). Although there is nothing wrong with spending the world currency, a time will come when political leaders will push for the use of microchip human implants as an alternative in the name of security. The process of implanting a chip into the right hand or forehead will become acceptable as a form of identification and commerce in the name of security, economic planning, and prosperity. This implant will be accomplished painlessly through laser technology. It will be voluntary at the initial stage and later mandatory like the Social Security number or identification card in many countries. People will be able to buy and sell by having the microchip implants on their right hands or foreheads scanned. This technology is what the Scriptures refer to as the *mark of the beast.* (Rev. 13:16-17)

Since the introduction of the one-world currency will be insidious, the persecution of the saints under this wave will be gradual. However, for those who are wise, this is the time to go underground and aggressively spread the gospel of our Lord Jesus Christ, for the time will be very short indeed. Cities of refuge will be provided by the Lord to the elects in the Western world and in countries that participate in the global currency. To those who refuse to take the mark of the beast and worship at the altar of materialism, humanism, and Satanism, the Lord will make a way of escape. The Lord will make the cities of refuge in those countries to be cities of light. This book is written for the patience and endurance of the saints. With the spread of the mark of the beast comes the narrowing of the field available for evangelism until the time given to the Gentiles is fulfilled.

Since Christians and Jews have been given very clear instruction not to participate in the cashless society through microchip implants, Christians worldwide will create resistance movements. Christians will fight evil to stand still and "overcome by the blood of Jesus Christ and by the word of their testimony for they loved not their lives unto the death" (Rev. 12:11). However, many will be jailed, tortured, and killed. This is to fulfill the Word of God as written in Revelation 6:9: "When he opened the fifth seal, I saw under the altar the souls of those who had been slain for the word of God and for the testimony which they held."

Third Wave of Tribulation: One-World Government

A man will arise in Germany who, along with the powerful leader of North America, will emerge as a great war hero of the World War III as discussed in chapter eight. This great German leader is described in the Scriptures as "the beast." This charismatic, intelligent, bold, and powerful leader from Germany will achieve in a short time what Hitler failed to accomplish, exercising political control over the whole world. This German will be the leader of the emerging new world order, a form of one-world government. The highlights of this one-world government will be global currency, microchip human implants, and attempts to forge a form of world religion.

The laws that are designed to make microchip human implant the legal tender in many countries will be a great blow to many Jews and Christians who have received clear instruction from God not to participate in the system. This new world order will drive many Christian movements underground, isolate many Jews, and make everyone who refuses to participate social outcasts in their own countries. What a great trial! What great tribulation! What great endurance will be required of the saints!

According to the Scriptures, the new world order will maintain absolute power over the world for forty-two months before the next event happens.

This is to fulfill the Word of God as written in Revelation:

> So they worshiped the dragon who gave authority to the beast; and they worshiped the beast, saying, "Who is like the beast? Who is able to make war with him?" And he was given a mouth speaking great things and blasphemies, and he was given authority to continue for forty-two months . . . All who dwell on the earth will worship him, whose names have not been written in the Book of Life of the Lamb slain from the foundation of the world . . . Here is the patience and the faith of the saints. (Rev. 13:4-10)

This leader of the coming new world order will wear down the saints and drive them into hiding. Hence, many Christians will come to the realization that this is indeed the last generation; this season is indeed the end time. This fire of tribulation will wake up many from their slumber and get them ready for the coming of the bridegroom. Jesus Christ is not coming for a weak and sick bride, but the one who is purged, cleansed, and ready.

This is to fulfill the Word of God:

> . . . for the marriage of the Lamb has come, and his wife has made herself ready. And to her it was granted to be arrayed in fine linen, clean and bright, for the fine linen is the righteous acts of the saints. (Rev. 19:7-8)

Fourth Wave of Tribulation: World Religion

Personal Insight: There will be a form of world religion in the future. This is another wave to be resisted by the followers of Jesus Christ.

During this wave of tribulation, there will be a mass exodus of Christians and Jews to thousands of cities of refuge worldwide that the Lord has set apart for the elect. Some of these cities will be in form of camps hurriedly set up to accommodate thousands of Christians looking for a place of refuge. Those who move to these cities will be saved from the great tribulation that will follow.

Peter, an apostle of our Lord Jesus Christ, gave the church a prophetic message regarding the severe and coming persecution of the Christian church.

> Beloved, do not think it strange concerning the fiery trial which is to try you . . . but rejoice to the extent that you partake of Christ's sufferings, that when his glory is revealed, you may also be glad with exceeding joy. (1 Pet. 4:12-13)

Chapter Ten

Fifth Seal Part II: Seven-Year Peace Treaty and the Great Tribulation (September 2022-2029 A.D.)

After a season of war, there will be a season of peace. After the World War III, a seven-year peace treaty will be signed by the warring factions. This treaty will be supported by a European leader (the beast) who is from Germany, supported by the leader of the United States (the false prophet) and an Arab leader (the little horn). A conference will be called by world leaders to proclaim peace. During this conference, an Arab prince will be seen working hard for peace. The outcome of this conference will be a seven-year treaty that will guarantee peace in the Middle East. This Arab prince is the little horn of the book of Daniel and the Assyrian of the book of Isaiah as discussed earlier. One of the significant issues of this treaty will be an attempt to make the Middle East a nuclear-weapon-free zone.

> Then he shall confirm a covenant with many for one week; but in the middle of the week he shall bring an end to sacrifice and offering (Dan. 9:27a).

Remember that in the prophetic scriptures, a day is often a year. The "day for a year" principle is in operation here. The little horn, the Assyrian, will come out with a seven-year peace treaty. The whole world will be deceived by this treaty and this prince may be honored with the Nobel Peace Prize.

However, in the middle of the week—that is, after three-and-one-half "days" (or years)—this Arab leader will violate the terms of the peace agreement and invade the Temple Mount and cause the daily sacrifices to stop. This invasion will lead to another war, abandonment of the Temple Mount by the Jews, and desolation of the eastern part of Jerusalem

Building of the Third Temple

After the destruction of the Dome of Rock, there will be a prophetic instruction to the Jews to build the house of the Lord. *The temple will be built on the same spot on which the Dome of Rock is standing now, most likely before 2029 A.D.* This will be a time of national revival among the Jews, and many shall return to the Lord; many shall be saved. The Lord will put the fear of them on their neighbors. Ironically, while the Jews will be building the temple, the Arabs will be preparing for war. The third temple in Jerusalem will be completed under the new and deceiving atmosphere of peace. Security measures will be relaxed by the Israel Defense Forces due to the existing seven-year peace treaty.

In recent years, the Temple Institute has been filing requests at Israel's Supreme Court to conduct animal sacrifices on the Temple Mount on the eve of Passover feasts. To date, such requests have been denied for security reasons, but the time is coming when the Temple Institute will take control of the Temple Mount. At that time, animal sacrifices will commence during morning and evening worship.

The Jews do not need the existence of a Temple to start the daily sacrifices. They only need a temporary altar set at a place chosen by the high priest and the accepted prophets of God. This daily animal sacrifices, as in the days of old, will continue until the third temple is completed.

Personal Insight: After the third temple might have been completed and during a great celebration, there will be a tragedy on the Temple Mount. There will be an attack by terrorists at the doorstep of the temple, and human blood shall flow. Just as Antiochus IV Epiphanes sacrificed swine on the altar to desecrate Solomon's Temple, men will commit ritual suicide on the Temple Mount and desecrate the temple with human blood. What a great attack against the Jews and the temple! This is the abomination that makes desolate. When this happens, Jesus Christ instructed the inhabitants of Jerusalem and neighboring towns to flee because a great war is coming. Another holocaust against the Jews will be launched. This is the advent of *the great tribulation.*

The cessation of daily sacrifices in the temple marks the beginning of the great tribulation:

> "Therefore when you see the 'abomination of desolation,' spoken of by Daniel the prophet, standing in the holy place" (whoever reads, let him understand), *"then let those who are in Judea flee to the mountains . . . For then there will be great tribulation, such as has not been since the beginning of the world until this time, no, nor ever shall be.* And unless those days were shortened, no flesh would be saved; but for the elect's sake those days will be shortened." (Matt 24:15-22, emphasis mine)

The Great Tribulation: Three-and-One-Half Years = 42 months = 1260 Days

"The little horn" of the prophet Daniel, referred to as "the Assyrian" by the prophet Isaiah, is the one responsible for the desecration of the temple of the living God. By uniting many countries in the Middle East to form a regional government, he will emerge as a powerful political figure in the whole of the Middle East. This regional government will use the European Union as a template and support the idea of a global currency for international trade.

Personal Insight: This emerging power bloc from the Middle East will ally with North African Arabs and China. The emerging Arab leader will be extremely corrupt, deceptive, dangerous, and aggressive. He will not care about the religion of his fathers, Islam, but will use it for his selfish political agenda. With his golden tongue, many will be deceived. He will be pro-West in order to prevent the West from actively defending the Jews. While talking about peace, he will use every opportunity to wage war. The ambition of the emerging regional government in the Middle East will be to rule the world and spread Islam to the rest of the world.

This will be a time of great tribulation and holocaust for the Jews. Two-thirds of the Jewish population will be killed. This will be the worst holocaust in the history of humanity—an attempt to annihilate the Jews completely and to take over their God-given land. Millions of Jews will die. This holocaust is prophetically described by Zechariah and Daniel.

> "And it shall come to pass in all the land," says the Lord, *"that two-thirds in it shall be cut off and die, but one-third shall be left in it: I will bring the one-third through the fire, will refine them as silver is refined, and test them as gold is tested.* They will call on my name, and I will answer them. I will say, 'This is my people'; and each one will say, 'The Lord is my God.'" (Zech. 13:8-9, emphasis mine)

> *"And those of the people who understand shall instruct many; yet for many days they shall fall by sword and flame, by captivity and plundering.* Now when they fall, they shall be aided with a little help; but many shall join with them by intrigue. *And some of those of understanding shall fall, to refine them, purify them, and make them white, until the time of the end;* because it is still for the appointed time." (Dan. 11:33-35, emphasis mine)

Hundreds of Jewish worshipers will be killed within the temple. When the temple is desecrated, it will bring sacrifice to an end. War will be waged because the peace treaty would have been violated. The cessation of the day and evening sacrifices on a day of great celebration in the temple marks the first day of the last three-and-one-half years preceding the coming of our Lord.

The Abomination that Makes Desolate: 2022-2029 A.D.

The cessation of morning and evening sacrifices is referred to as an *abomination*. This will lead to war, which will bring desolation to part of Jerusalem; hence the phrase "abomination that makes desolate." This is the last major event preceding the second coming of our Lord Jesus Christ. Our Lord Jesus Christ wants us to watch carefully for this event.

> "Therefore when you see the 'abomination of desolation,' spoken of by Daniel the prophet, standing in the holy place" (whoever reads, let him understand), then let those who are in Judea flee to the mountains." (Matt. 24:15-16)

In his statement, Jesus Christ affirmed the vision and prophecy of Daniel regarding this same abomination of desolation.

> Then I, Daniel, looked; and there stood two others, one on this riverbank and the other on that riverbank. And one said to the man clothed in linen, who was above the waters of the river, "How long shall the fulfillment of these wonders be?" Then I heard the man clothed in linen, who was above the waters of the river, when he held up his right hand and his left hand to heaven, and swore by him who lives forever, that it shall be for a time, times, and half a time; and *when the power of the holy people has been completely shattered,*

all these things shall be finished . . . And from the time that the daily sacrifice is taken away, and the abomination of desolation is set up, there shall be one thousand two hundred and ninety days. Blessed is he who waits, and comes to the one thousand three hundred and thirty-five days. But you, go your way till the end; for you shall rest, and will arise to your inheritance at the end of the days." (Dan. 12:4-13, emphasis mine)

Daniel gave a very objective description of the span of the great tribulation. Although in many parts of the Scriptures, it is referred to as three-and-one-half years or forty-two months, the prophet Daniel gave the actual number of days between the cessation of sacrifices in the temple and the end of the great tribulation that will ensue. According to Daniel, we need to count between *1260 and 1335 days, both days inclusive. By 1335 days, the mystery of the rapture/resurrection of the dead will have been completed.*

The lifespan of this end-time generation will not go beyond 1335 days from the cessation of the animal sacrifice on the Temple Mount.

The Prophet Daniel's Significant Period

All the dates are referenced from the cessation of temple sacrifice in Jerusalem. The first date: 1260 days; the second date: 1290 days; the third date: 1335 days.

1. Daniel 12:7 gives "a time, times, and half a time" = 1 year + 2 years + ½ year = 3 1/2 years = 42 months = 42×30 days = 1260 days.

   "Then I heard the man clothed in linen, who was above the waters of the river, when he held up his right hand and his left hand to heaven, and swore by him who lives forever, that it shall be for *a time, times, and half a time;* and when the power of the holy people has been completely shattered, all these things shall be finished." (emphasis mine).

2. Daniel 12:11 gives 1290 days.

    "And from the time that the daily sacrifice is taken away, and the abomination of desolation is set up, *there shall be one thousand two hundred and ninety days.*" (emphasis mine).

3. Daniel 12:12 gives 1335 days.

    "Blessed is he who waits, and comes to the one thousand three hundred and thirty-five days."

By not giving a specific date for the end time but a time period between *1260 days and 1335 days post cessation of temple sacrifices,* Daniel reaffirms the words of Jesus Christ (Matt. 24:36) that no one knows the date or the hour that the second coming/rapture will take place.

Life Span of the Last Generation (1948-2029)

A generation does not run indefinitely; therefore, the last generation has a life span. There are scriptural references regarding this. According to the book of Psalms, the time limit for a generation is eighty years. (Psalm 90:10, 12)

This prophetic utterance is very relevant to this generation because the last ten years will be characterized by labor and sorrow, especially among the true Christians in the Middle East and Western nations.

We need to understand that the Hebrew calendar is different from our modern Gregorian calendar. While the modern calendar starts from January, Hebrew's New Year always starts from September/October at the feast of Rosh Hashanah. By using this understanding to calculate the life span of this generation, we end up with 1948 + 80 years = 2028/2029. The last ten years of this life span will be

2028/2029 minus 10 years = 2018/2019. Therefore, this decade—2018/2019 to 2028/2029—will be very significant in the program of God. During this decade, a form of global currency, world religion, and world government will be formed. Moreover, the emergence of a new world order will usher in the persecution of Christians in Europe and then worldwide.

Since we are the last generation, many rapid changes will occur between now and 2029, changes that will usher in waves of tribulation for the Jews and the saints in Christ. Moreover, we need to watch for the invasion of Turkey because the consequence of the Russian invasion of that country will be felt around the world. Men and women of God moved by the Holy Spirit will declare to the world what is about to take place. The good news is that the Lord has chosen nations that will receive refugees migrating from the Middle East, Europe, and North America until the time the evil of the World War III might have passed. This is why we need to watch and pray.

The United States

During the period of the great tribulation of the Jews, the United States will come to the aid of Israel and airlift many to safety. This is highlighted in the book of Revelation. (Rev. 12:1, 5-6, 13-14)

There was war in heaven, and the devil-the enemy of our souls-was cast down to the earth. Knowing that his time is short he persecuted Israel, which is represented by the woman clothed with the sun, with the moon under her feet, and on her head a garland of twelve stars (twelve tribes). Jesus Christ is the son of God given through the nation Israel, who is going to rule all nations with a rod of iron. The wrath of the devil will be poured upon Israel because she gave birth to Jesus Christ, the one who will destroy the devil and rule the world. Giving birth to Jesus Christ made the devil, the ancient serpent, go after Israel to annihilate her. This is the great tribulation.

The agents of the devil are the beast (the German leader); the false prophet (the North American leader); and the little horn (the Arab leader). These three are the authors of the seven-year peace treaty; a deceptive peace treaty that gives Israel a false sense of security and makes her very vulnerable to attack.

When the Arab leader brings about the end of the daily sacrifices and commits the abomination that makes desolate that gives birth to the great tribulation, the woman will be given two wings of *a great eagle*. This symbolizes the United States coming to help the Jews by airlifting many to safety. Many Jews will escape to Petra, a city built into the slope of Mount Hor. Some Jews will escape through Greece to Europe, while others will escape to some African countries. By the power of God, the Jews will not be annihilated. Therefore, the devil is angry and goes after United States for coming to the aid of Israel.

> And the dragon was enraged with the woman, and he went to make war with the rest of her offspring, who keep the commandments of God and have the testimony of Jesus Christ. (Rev. 12:17)

For this reason, the United States (especially the New York City, being the second largest Jewish population center in the world after the Tel Aviv Metropolitan Area) will be attacked by terrorists using both nuclear and biological weapons.

Worst Terrorist Attack in Human History Against New York City

Personal Insight: After the commencement of the great tribulation, terrorists will attack the United States, and New York City will be hit. This will be a revenge attack for coming to the aid of Israel during the time of the great tribulation. This attack will take place in New York City harbor after the temple in Jerusalem had been built and after the celebrated Arab leader has rebelled against world

111

rulers by attacking the Jews and bringing animal sacrifices on the Temple Mount to an end.

Manhattan will become an epicenter of nuclear explosion. However, this will be nothing compared to a biological virus that will be released at this time. This bioterrorism will cause a fatal flu-like syndrome that will kill millions of people in a short time. The whole of New York City will be shut down by the Department of Health in order to quarantine people and prevent the spread of the fatal and contagious disease.

This shall be the sign that bioterrorism has occurred and that people must move out of New York City as soon as possible within twenty-four hours: when the Statue of Liberty is destroyed by a bomb.

New York City has been marked for divine judgment. A time will come when the people of God must leave the city so that they will not share in her plagues, for in one hour her plague will come from her harbor. When you see the Statue of Liberty bombed, her plague has come.

> And I heard another voice from heaven saying, "Come out of her, my people, lest you share in her sins, and lest you receive of her plagues. For her sins have reached to heaven, and God has remembered her iniquities . . . Therefore her plagues will come in one day—death and mourning and famine. And she will be utterly burned with fire, for strong is the Lord God who judges her." (Rev. 18:4-10)

Revelation 18:4 will be fulfilled during the great tribulation. "And I heard another voice from heaven saying, "Come out of her, my people, lest you share in her sins, and lest you receive of her plagues." The people of God in New York City need to pay attention to what will be happening in Jerusalem after the building of the third temple and prepare to move out of the city when the Statue of Liberty is destroyed.

Two Great Prophets

During the period of the great tribulation lasting about three-and-one-half years, two great prophets of God will become known worldwide. These two end-time prophets will be anointed by the Holy Spirit to bring about repentance and great revival among the Jews and turn their hearts to Jesus Christ. Through their ministries, many Jews shall accept Jesus Christ as their savior and give their hearts to him. (Rev. 11:1-6)

These two prophets will prophesy in black cloth for three-and-one-half years; their ministries will receive worldwide attention when the Temple Mount is forcefully taken over and the daily sacrifice is brought to an end. These two men will lead both the Christian church and the Jewish nation in taking the gospel to the ends of the earth. There will be many attempts to kill them, but their enemies will be divinely judged and destroyed. These two men and their followers will be a shining light to the dying world. Great signs and wonders will be done through the ministries of these great servants of God. This is the grace of God calling men and women to repent and escape from the wrath of God that is coming. Will the people listen?

These two prophets will be hated because they will proclaim that the wrath of God is coming and challenge the world to repent. They will reject the growing one-world government; condemn the enlarging ecumenical council; and prophetically declare destruction on anyone participating in the one-world, cashless currency. Like John the Baptist, these will address the masses, the soldiers, and the political leaders. Truth is bitter and the Word of God is sharp—sharper than any two-edged sword. Therefore, their prophetic declaration of the coming judgment of God will put them in the class of prophets of doom. The divine intervention of God in Israel via these two prophets will allow one-third of the Jews to escape death and prevent the western part of Jerusalem from falling completely into the hands of the Arabs. For 1260 days—that is, throughout the entire period of the great tribulation—these men will declare the undiluted Word of God and give guidance to the church and the Jews.

They have power to shut heaven so that no rain falls in the days of their prophecy, creating a severe, worldwide drought. Just as in the days of Elijah, this is part of a divine judgment for the idolatry of humanity. Even many rivers will become red and undrinkable as a result of the severe drought. This will be a very dry season worldwide. Many people will thirst for both natural water and the spiritual water of life. Those countries in low rainfall regions will experience great drought. Many lakes and rivers will dry up. The prophets will also prophesy about the flu-like syndrome that will kill *millions of people*. These men will prophesy about the coming wrath of God and encourage people to escape and be saved in Christ Jesus. Will the people listen? These two prophets will lead the *last phase of the end time global revival.*

The Two Great Prophets Will Be Killed

When they finish their testimony, the beast that ascends out of the bottomless pit will make war against them, *overcome them, and kill them*. And their dead bodies will lie in the street of the great city which spiritually is called Sodom and Egypt, where also our Lord was crucified. Then those from the peoples, tribes, tongues, and nations will see their dead bodies three-and-a-half days, and not allow their dead bodies to be put into graves. And those who dwell on the earth will rejoice over them, make merry, and send gifts to one another, because these two prophets tormented those who dwell on the earth. (Rev. 11:7-10, emphasis mine)

Immediately after the great tribulation—that is, after 1260-1335 days—having finished their testimony, these two great leaders of the Jews and the Christian church will be killed in the streets of Jerusalem. Many people worldwide will rejoice because, for them, the prophets of doom have been killed. For three days, the whole world will watch the dead bodies of these men in Jerusalem via satellite and cable networks. *The death of these two powerful prophets of God marks the end of the three-and-one-half years of tribulation of the saints and the beginning of the awesome display of the power and the glory of Christ Jesus in the heavenlies.*

Resurrection Cometh!

But the prophets do not stay dead on the street. God has a surprise for the world that is rejoicing over their death:

> Now after the three-and-a-half days the breath of life from God entered them, and they stood on their feet, and great fear fell on those who saw them. And they heard a loud voice from heaven saying to them, "Come up here." And they ascended to heaven in a cloud, and their enemies saw them. In the same hour there was a great earthquake, and a tenth of the city fell. In the earthquake seven thousand people were killed, and the rest were afraid and gave glory to the God of heaven. (Rev. 11:11-13)

The Resurrection of the Two Witnesses = The Rapture/Resurrection of the Saints

Immediately after the tribulation of those days (lasting between 1260 and 1335 days from the cessation of the daily sacrifice)—the two witnesses will be killed on the streets of Jerusalem, resulting in breaking news worldwide. For three-and-one-half days, their dead bodies will lie on the street; their enemies will not allow their bodies to be put into graves.

After three-and-one-half days, something strange will happen. The glory of Jesus Christ will be seen in the heavens and the breath of life from God will enter the two witnesses and they will stand on their feet. Those who see them will be overwhelmed by fear, and there will be a loud voice from heaven like a loud trumpet blast saying to them, "Come up here." They will ascend to heaven in a cloud leading the *great assembly onto Mount Zion for the marriage supper of the Lamb*. Following their resurrection, there will be a great *resurrection earthquake* that will affect many nations, and a tenth of Jerusalem will be affected. In Jerusalem alone, seven thousand people will die in the earthquake.

Those who have died in Christ Jesus, including the two great prophets, will be resurrected while those who are alive will be transformed in the twinkling of an eye to be caught up unto the Lord in heaven. This is the first resurrection.

> Behold, I tell you a mystery: We shall not all sleep, but we shall all be changed—in a moment, in the twinkling of an eye, at the last trumpet. For the trumpet will sound, and the dead will be raised incorruptible, and we shall be changed. (1 Cor. 15:51)

> And I saw thrones, and they sat on them, and judgment was committed to them. Then I saw the souls of those who had been beheaded for their witness to Jesus and for the word of God, who had not worshiped the beast or his image, and had not received his mark on their foreheads or on their hands. And they lived and reigned with Christ for a thousand years. But the rest of the dead did not live again until the thousand years were finished. This is the first resurrection. (Rev. 20:4-5)

Whosoever misses the rapture (which occurs with the first resurrection) will not take part in the marriage supper of the Lamb and in the millennial reign of Jesus Christ (one thousand years of peace) but will go through the wrath of God that will come upon everyone who misses the rapture.

Chapter Eleven

Sixth Seal: The Rapture and the Marriage Supper of the Lamb

"Immediately after the tribulation of those days the *sun will be darkened*, and the moon will not give its light; the *stars will fall from heaven*, and the powers of the heavens will be shaken. Then the sign of the Son of Man will appear in heaven, and then all the tribes of the earth will mourn, and they will see the Son of Man coming on the clouds of heaven with power and great glory. And he will send his angels with a great *sound of a trumpet*, and they will *gather together his elect* from the four winds, from one end of heaven to the other." (Matt. 24:29-31, emphasis mine)

Rapture Events

1. Immediately after the tribulation of those days—*that is, after three-and-one-half years of the cessation of daily sacrifices* in the temple—something profound will happen. (Matt. 24:29a)
2. There will be a great eclipse because a great comet will come between the sun and the earth; therefore *the sun will be darkened* and *the moon will not give its light*. The sudden appearance of the glory and power of Jesus Christ in heaven is going to be referred to as *an unusual comet*. (Matt. 24:29a)
3. This great light that appears as a comet is the sign of the Son of Man. It will display the awesomeness

of the power and the glory of Jesus Christ. The appearance of this light will be followed by *a great explosion* that will shake the heavens and give rise to meteorite showers. People all over the world will wonder at the heavenly display of the power of God. *This is what the Scripture calls "the loud trumpet blast."* The great heavenly explosion also causes the earth to tremble, which will lead to *earthquakes in numerous places.* Numerous meteorite showers will shoot out from the comet appearing as *millions of stars falling from heaven.* (Matt. 24: 29b-30)

4. The Lord will send his angels, and they will gather together his elect from the four winds, from one end of heaven to the other. This will occur even before the meteorite showers hit the earth's surface. (Matt. 24:31)

5. The appearance of the Lord will coincide with the destruction of the little horn, who has taken control of the temple of the Lord. Not by power, not by might, but by the Word of God, the man of lawlessness will be destroyed. This is to fulfill the Scriptures in 2 Thessalonians 2:8: "And then the lawless one will be revealed, whom the Lord will consume with the breath of his mouth and destroy with the brightness of his coming."

6. The end of the beast (the European leader) and the false prophet (the North American leader) will be discussed during the seventh trumpet of judgment in chapter thirteen of this book.

The Sign of the Glory of the Lord

I looked when he opened the sixth seal, and behold, there was a great earthquake; and the sun became black as sackcloth of hair, and the moon became like blood. And the stars of heaven fell to the earth, as a fig tree drops its late figs when it is shaken by a mighty wind. (Rev. 6:12-13)

> The sun shall be turned into darkness, and the moon into blood, before the coming of the great and awesome day of the Lord. (Joel 2:31)

What the scientists will call a great and strange comet is the appearance of the sign of the glory of the Lord Jesus Christ.

The Word of God guarantees that the elect will never participate in the wrath of God. Since the day of the rapture is the day that the wrath of God is revealed, the elect are sealed before the natural disasters that accompany the rapture event strike.

The Rapture: Noah's Ark

The rapture is designed by the living God to save the elect, the people of God, from the wrath of God that is about to be unleashed on the inhabitants of the world. This is to fulfill the Word of God:

> For God did not appoint us to wrath, but to obtain salvation through our Lord Jesus Christ. (1 Thess. 5:9)

After the rapture, there will be three great natural disasters that will be discussed in this and the next chapter. These disasters will be global in impact. The severity and destructive nature of these disasters are beyond imagination. Great misery, unbearable suffering, and heart-wrenching calamities will visit the earth. Moreover, after the rapture, there will be a world war that will claim billions of lives (Rev. 9:18). The Lord Jesus Christ does not want us to go through this excruciating judgment. That is why we need to make a decision today. We need to repent from our old ways, confess our sins to the Lord, invite Jesus Christ into our hearts by faith, and experience the transformative power of the Holy Spirit.

The rapture is our Noah's Ark. On the day that the Lord has chosen, everyone whose name is written in the book of life will be caught up into the air. Then the wrath of God will be revealed upon those who are left behind.

This is why the prophet Isaiah made a proclamation that the resurrection of the dead shall be followed by the wrath of God. The people of God will be hidden in heaven while the wrath of God is unleashed upon the earth. (Isa. 26:19-21)

Those who are left behind will face a grim future, one characterized by the fierce anger of Almighty God. The wrath of God will conclude with a great flood. It will be like in the days of Noah. To escape, the only thing we need to do is to come to Jesus Christ. He is the way, the truth and the life; no one can come to the Heavenly father but by him. (John 14:6)

The Marriage Supper of the Lamb

Immediately after the rapture and the resurrection of the saints, two things will happen simultaneously. Those who are caught up to be with the Lord will be at the marriage supper of the Lamb, while those who are left behind on earth will face the wrath of God. There are only two options available to every inhabitant of the earth: celebrate the marriage supper of the Lamb in heaven or face the wrath of God on earth. Therefore, to miss the rapture is to miss the marriage supper of the Lamb; to miss the rapture is to face the wrath of God. There are no other options. People of God, we have to be watchful and vigilant lest we are distracted by the lust of this world, the lust of flesh, and the pride of life—lest we become lukewarm in our spiritual lives.

Breaking News

On the day of rapture, there will be three major events impacting the whole world. Breaking news on major satellite and cable networks will report these events.

- The resurrection of two renowned prophets of God on the streets of Jerusalem and their bodily ascension into heaven.
- The sudden disappearance of millions of people all over the world.
- Great earthquakes affecting many cities of the world at the same time.

> In the same hour there was a great earthquake, and a tenth of the city fell. In the earthquake seven thousand people were killed, and the rest were afraid and gave glory to the God of heaven. (Rev. 11:13)

The sudden disappearance of the saints of God will mark the beginning of the wrath of God. The disappearance of pilots will suddenly lead to airplanes crashing and the disappearance of the drivers of automobiles will cause highway accidents all over the world. Surgeons will disappear during surgical procedures; midwives will disappear during labor delivery; army generals will disappear from their posts. Can you imagine nurses, pastors, lawyers, bankers, teachers, babysitters, children, wives, husbands, musicians, political leaders, traders, artists, actors, actresses, engineers, police officers, soldiers, servants, slaves, prisoners, managers, supervisors, employers, employees, singles, homeless, and union workers all disappearing suddenly? What a great crisis! What a great challenge to those who are left behind! This is likely to be the worst crisis humanity has ever faced since the day of creation. Unfortunately, this is just the beginning of the wrath of God. *A greater crisis comes.*

God's Wrath

God's wrath will start on the day of resurrection. The earth will be shaken. There will be so many earthquakes all over the globe that people will hide in caves and secured places in order to be saved.

> Then the sky receded as a scroll when it is rolled up, and every mountain and island was moved out of its place. And the kings of the earth, the great men, the rich men, the commanders, the mighty men, every slave and every free man, hid themselves in the caves and in the rocks of the mountains, and said to the mountains and rocks, "Fall on us and hide us from the face of him who sits on the throne and from the wrath of the Lamb! For the great day of his wrath has come, and who is able to stand?" (Rev. 6: 14-17)

Great severe earthquakes will affect many cities of the world. Jerusalem and certain cities in the state of California will be involved. Great skyscrapers will collapse like toys. California will be so affected that it will bring United States to her knees economically. The San Andreas Fault will be affected. Yuri Fialko's prediction will come to pass.

Professor Yuri Fialko of the Scripps Institution of Oceanography at the University of California, San Diego completed a study that demonstrated that the San Andreas Fault has been stressed to a level sufficient for the next "big one" (as it is commonly called)—that is, an earthquake of magnitude 7.0 or greater.[14] The study also concluded that the risk of a large earthquake may be increasing faster than researchers had previously believed. Fialko also emphasized that, while the San Andreas Fault had experienced massive earthquakes in 1857 at its central section and in 1906 at its northern segment (the 1906 San Francisco earthquake),

---

[14] http://phys.org/news70114196.html (last accessed June 21, 2012)

the southern section of the fault has not seen a similar rupture in at least three hundred years.

If such an earthquake were to occur, Fialko's study stated, it would result in substantial damage to Palm Springs and a number of other cities in San Bernardino, Riverside, and Imperial counties in California, as well as the Mexicali municipality in Baja, California. Such an event would be felt throughout much of Southern California, including the densely populated areas of metropolitan Los Angeles, Orange County, San Diego and Tijuana, and Baja.

"The information available suggests that the fault is ready for the next big earthquake but exactly when the triggering will happen and when the earthquake will occur we cannot tell. It could be tomorrow or it could be 10 years or more from now," Fialko concluded in September 2005.

On the day of rapture, the big California earthquake will occur and Professor Fialko's prediction will come to pass. This earthquake will be so severe that it will be accompanied by volcanic eruption in some places. All earthquake-prone places on the Planet Earth will be affected. For the United States and other affected nations, the cost of rebuilding destroyed cities will overwhelm their economies. Many nations will go bankrupt. As a result, many banks and financial institutions will close. Famine, starvation, pestilence, inflation, and lawlessness will follow. There will be riots in many cities. Malls, stores, shops, and good-looking houses will be broken into by people looking for means of survival. Socio-political and economic structures will be turned upside-down. Human life will lose value. Some countries will experience violent revolutions. Socialists will revolt against capitalists in many countries. Prevailing social unrest in Europe and the United States will help the beast and the false prophet to use martial law to consolidate their political power. Many world leaders will be looking for scapegoats for the natural disasters. False prophets and politicians with deceitful tongues will use the great crisis for their selfish ends. Many fingers will be pointed at Israel. Why? The Jewish nation produced the two powerful prophets of God, who had prophesied for forty-two months regarding the worldwide earthquake.

Greater Trouble Comes

- A few hours/days later, the shooting stars—the meteors—will be striking many places on the earth. See the first trumpet discussion in the next chapter.
- Days later, a great mountain burning with fire will be cast into the sea. See the second trumpet discussion in the next chapter.

Chapter Twelve

Seventh Seal Part I:
The Wrath of God

> When he opened the seventh seal, there was
> silence in heaven for about half an hour. (Rev. 8:1)

The prophet Zephaniah warned about the coming wrath of
God:

> The great day of the Lord is near; it is near and
> hastens quickly. The noise of the day of the Lord
> is bitter; there the mighty men shall cry out.
> That day is a day of wrath, a day of trouble and
> distress, a day of devastation and desolation, a
> day of darkness and gloominess, a day of clouds
> and thick darkness, a day of trumpet and alarm
> against the fortified cities and against the high
> towers. "I will bring distress upon men, and they
> shall walk like blind men, because they have
> sinned against the Lord; their blood shall be
> poured out like dust, and their flesh like refuse."
> (Zeph. 1:14-17)

The prophet Isaiah also prophesied about the coming wrath
of God.

> Behold, the day of the Lord comes, cruel, with both
> wrath and fierce anger, to lay the land desolate;
> and he will destroy its sinners from it. For the

stars of heaven and their constellations will not give their light; the sun will be darkened in its going forth, and the moon will not cause its light to shine. I will punish the world for its evil, and the wicked for their iniquity . . . Therefore I will shake the heavens, and the earth will move out of her place, in the wrath of the Lord of hosts and in the day of his fierce anger. (Isa. 13:9-13)

The Wrath: Seven Trumpets and Seven Vials

The wrath of God will be poured out on the inhabitants of the world left behind after the rapture. In the book of Revelation, this wrath is described using two symbols: the trumpets and the vials. By paying attention to the word of God, we understand that both the seven trumpets of wrath and the seven vials of wrath are describing the same events. The doubling of the events in the book of Revelation shows the certainty of the wrath of God.

We see a similar biblical reference when Pharaoh had two dreams pointing to the same event—seven years of famine. In Genesis 41:32 Joseph said to Pharaoh, "And the dream was repeated to Pharaoh twice because the thing is established by God, and God will shortly bring it to pass." Since the vision is doubled in the book of Revelation, it is because the thing is established by God, and God will shortly bring it to pass.

Let us compare the trumpet judgments with the vial judgments and see the relationship between the two. In this chapter, we will discuss the first and second judgments upon the inhabitants of the earth left behind after the rapture. The remaining five trumpet judgments will be examined in the next chapter.

Book of Revelation Chapters 8, 9 Trumpet Judgments	Book of Revelation Chapters 15, 16 Vial (Bowl) Judgments
Introduction: Heavenly Temple Filled with God's Glory And I saw the seven angels who stand before God, and to them were given seven trumpets. Then another angel, having a golden censer, came and stood at the altar. He was given much incense, that he should offer it with the prayers of all the saints upon the golden altar which was before the throne. *And the smoke of the incense, with the prayers of the saints, ascended before God from the angel's hand.* (Rev. 8:2-4, emphasis mine)	**Introduction: Heavenly Temple Filled with God's Glory** Then one of the four living creatures gave to the seven angels seven golden bowls full of the wrath of God who lives forever and ever. *The temple was filled with smoke from the glory of God and from his power, and no one was able to enter the temple till the seven plagues of the seven angels were completed.* (Rev. 15:7-8, emphasis mine)
First Trumpet: Effects of Divine Fire on Plants and Animals The first angel sounded: And hail and fire followed, mingled with blood, and they were thrown to the earth. *And a third of the trees were burned up, and all green grass was burned up.* (Rev. 8:7, emphasis mine)	**First Vial (Bowl): Effects of Divine Fire on Human Skin** So the first went and poured out his bowl upon the earth, and *a foul and loathsome sore* came upon the men who had the mark of the beast and those who worshiped his image. (Rev. 16:2, emphasis mine)
Second Trumpet: Bloody Sea Then the second angel sounded: And something like a great mountain burning with fire was thrown into the *sea, and a third of the sea became blood.* And a third of the living creatures in the sea died, and a third of the ships were destroyed. (Rev. 8:8-9, emphasis mine)	**Second Vial (Bowl): Bloody Sea** Then the second angel poured out his bowl on the sea, *and it became blood* as of a dead man; and every living creature in the sea died. (Rev. 16:3, emphasis mine)

Third Trumpet: Judgments on Rivers and Springs	Third Vial (Bowl): Judgments on Rivers and Springs
Then the third angel sounded: And a great star fell from heaven, burning like a torch, and it fell *on a third of the rivers and on the springs of water.* The name of the star is Wormwood. A third of the waters became wormwood, and many men died from the water, because it was made bitter. (Rev. 8:10-11, emphasis mine)	Then the third angel poured out his bowl on the *rivers and springs of water,* and they became blood rivers. (Rev. 16:4, emphasis mine)
Fourth Trumpet: Sun Is Affected	**Fourth Vial (Bowl): Sun Is Affected**
Then the fourth angel sounded: *And a third of the sun was struck,* a third of the moon, and a third of the stars, so that a third of them were darkened. A third of the day did not shine, and likewise the night. (Rev. 8:12, emphasis mine)	Then the fourth angel *poured out his bowl on the sun,* and power was given to him to scorch men with fire. (Rev. 16:8, emphasis mine)
Fifth Trumpet: Darkness	**Fifth Vial (Bowl): Darkness**
Then the fifth angel sounded: And I saw a star fallen from heaven to the earth. To him was given the key to the bottomless pit. And he opened the bottomless pit, and smoke arose out of the pit like the smoke of a great furnace. *So the sun and the air were darkened because of the smoke of the pit.* Then out of the smoke locusts came upon the earth. And to them was given power, as the scorpions of the earth have power. (Rev. 9:1-3, emphasis mine)	Then the fifth angel poured out his bowl on the throne of the beast, *and his kingdom became full of darkness;* and they gnawed their tongues because of the pain. (Rev. 16:10, emphasis mine)

Sixth Trumpet: From Great River Euphrates to Armageddon	Sixth Vial (Bowl): From Great River Euphrates to Armageddon
Then the sixth angel sounded: And I heard a voice from the four horns of the golden altar which is before God, saying to the sixth angel who had the trumpet, "Release the four angels who are bound at the *great river Euphrates.*" So the four angels, who had been prepared for the hour and day and month and year, were released to kill a third of mankind. Now the number of the army of the horsemen was two hundred million; I heard the number of them. And thus I saw the horses in the vision: those who sat on them had breastplates of fiery red, hyacinth blue, and sulfur yellow; and the heads of the horses were like the heads of lions; and out of their mouths came fire, smoke, and brimstone. By these three plagues a third of mankind was killed—by the fire and the smoke and the brimstone which came out of their mouths. (Rev. 9:13-18, emphasis mine)	Then the sixth angel poured out his bowl on the *great river Euphrates,* and its water was dried up, so that the way of the kings from the east might be prepared And I saw three unclean spirits like frogs coming out of the mouth of the dragon, out of the mouth of the beast, and out of the mouth of the false prophet. For they are spirits of demons, performing signs, which go out to the kings of the earth and of the whole world, to gather them to the battle of that great day of God Almighty. "Behold, I am coming as a thief. Blessed is he who watches, and keeps his garments, lest he walk naked and they see his shame." And they gathered them together to the place called in Hebrew, Armageddon. (Rev. 16:12-16, emphasis mine)
Seventh Trumpet: Thundering, Lightning, and Earthquake	**Seventh Vial (Bowl): Thundering, Lightning, and Earthquake**
Then the seventh angel sounded: *And there were loud voices in heaven,* saying, "The kingdoms of this world have become the kingdoms of our Lord and of his Christ, and	Then the seventh angel poured out his bowl into the air, *and a loud voice came out of the temple of heaven,* from the throne, saying, "It is done!" *And there were noises and*

he shall reign forever and ever!" . . . Then the temple of God was opened in heaven, and the ark of his covenant was seen in his temple. *And there were lightnings, noises, thunderings, an earthquake, and great hail.* (Rev. 11:15, 19, emphasis mine)	*thunderings and lightnings; and there was a great earthquake, such a mighty and great earthquake as had not occurred since men were on the earth.* Now the great city was divided into three parts, and the cities of the nations fell . . . Then every island fled away, and the mountains were not found. And great hail from heaven fell upon men, each hailstone about the weight of a talent. Men blasphemed God because of the plague of the hail, since that plague was exceedingly great. (Rev. 16:17-21, emphasis mine)

The comparison of the seven trumpets and the seven bowls of judgment shows that both are projecting the same message. The first two judgments, which we are going to focus on in this chapter, declare two great natural disasters that are coming after the rapture.

First Trumpet Judgment = First Vial (Bowl) Judgment

First Trumpet: Effects of Divine Fire on Plants and Animals	First Vial (Bowl): Effects of Divine Fire on Human's Skin
The first angel sounded: And hail and fire followed, mingled with blood, and they were thrown to the earth. *And a third of the trees were burned up, and all green grass was burned up.* (Rev. 8:7, emphasis mine)	So the first went and poured out his bowl upon the earth, and *a foul and loathsome sore* came upon the men who had the mark of the beast and those who worshiped his image. (Rev. 16:2, emphasis mine)

Meteorite Shower

There will be a great explosion in the heavens, and millions of meteorites will fall like stars. This meteorite shower will rain stones and fire upon one-third of the earth. It shall be like in the time of biblical Sodom and Gomorrah-some cities will be completely ruined. The whole world will be stunned, and all eyes will turn to the sky to look at fire raining down on the inhabitants of the earth. This is to fulfill the Word of God:

> "Immediately after the tribulation of those days the sun will be darkened, and the moon will not give its light; *the stars will fall from heaven*, and the powers of the heavens will be shaken." (Matt. 24:29, emphasis mine)

> *And the stars of heaven fell to the earth*, as a fig tree drops its late figs when it is shaken by a mighty wind. (Rev. 6:13, emphasis mine)

There will be a global panic at this strange event. Many people will be scared to death, while others will be overwhelmed by feelings of hopelessness and helplessness. Many will run into holes in rock and caves, and many government officials will hide in secret, fortified underground cities. Many people will be wearing helmets for protection. Code disaster will be raised in many countries of the world.

Many great farms will be completely destroyed; vegetation around the world will lie in ruin. There will be great economic crisis. Great famine, worldwide in nature, will ensue. Prices of basic food commodities like rice, bread, corn, and milk will go up astronomically.

Worldwide Famine

Personal Insight: As a result of the hail and fire from heaven, there will be worldwide famine. It will be so severe that some will become cannibals. Survival will be the priority of many. Poverty levels will increase in many nations. Lawlessness, violence, and social vices will be common. Some great prosperous cities and nations will be brought down. Money will be useless; there will be hyperinflation. There will be epidemic of diseases due to malnutrition and depressed immunity. The kingdom of the beast and the false prophet will be greatly affected.

Mild to Severe Burns

Due to fire falling from heaven, hospital emergency rooms will be filled with those with various degrees of burns. Emergency burn centers will be set up in affected countries. *Infected wounds will present with foul-smelling discharges, fulfilling the Word of God in Revelation 16:2:* "So the first went and poured out his bowl upon the earth, and *a foul and loathsome sore* came upon the men who had the mark of the beast and those who worshiped his image." (Rev. 16:2) The health system will be overwhelmed. Due to the many injuries from falling stones, many centers for blood donation will be opened.

Second Trumpet Judgment = Second Bowl Judgment

Second Trumpet: Bloody Sea	Second Vial (Bowl): Bloody Sea
Then the second angel sounded: And something like a great mountain burning with fire was thrown into the sea, *and a third of the sea became blood.* And a third of the living creatures in the sea died, and a third of the ships were destroyed. (Rev. 8:8-9, emphasis mine)	Then the second angel poured out his bowl on the sea, *and it became blood* as of a dead man; and every living creature in the sea died.(Rev. 16:3, emphasis mine)

The second natural disaster after the rapture will be a great mountain (asteroid) thrown into a great sea. This will cause flooding in many major cities around the world.

Identification of the Sea

There are three major oceans in the world, but the one the Scripture is referring to makes up one-third of the oceans.

1. Pacific Ocean	169,200,000 sq km
2. Atlantic Ocean	106,400,000 sq km
3. Indian Ocean	73,556,000 sq km
Total	349,156,000 sq km

It is very clear from this data that the Atlantic Ocean makes up about one-third of the world's sea volume. *Therefore, the great mountain burning with fire will be thrown into the Atlantic Ocean.*

Greatest Tsunami of the Twenty-First Century

This great mountain of fire (asteroid) thrown into the Atlantic Ocean will cause the greatest tsunami of the twenty-first century. Immediately after the burning mountain (asteroid) hits, a dome of water almost three thousand feet high and tens of miles wide will form, only to collapse and rebound. Travelling at the speed of a jet aircraft, the great wave will smash into many coastal cities in Europe, America, North Africa, and West Sahara. Such a wave would travel about five miles inland, flattening everything in its path. Navigation and commerce will be severely disrupted. Virginia and all of the Gulf states will be flooded. The Mississippi River will experience great flood along its border, affecting Missouri, Illinois, and Minneapolis. New York City will be devastated. Skyscrapers will collapse like toys. Florida will be hit. The damage will be so severe that the NASA base will be affected. The province of Quebec in Canada will be destroyed. North and South America will not be able to restore what has been damaged or destroyed. The Western Sahara, Morocco, Portugal, Spain, France, and parts of the United Kingdom will also be hit. Through the Mediterranean and Black seas, southern Russia will be affected.

The destructive wave will pass through the coast of Germany to the Baltic Sea from where it will pass to the Gulf of Finland and Bothnia. The Aland Islands will be severely affected. Finland will be more affected than Sweden. A wall of water higher than Nelson's Column in London's Trafalgar Square will smash into the coasts of the Caribbean Islands. The northern coast of Brazil will be hit. A destructive wave will hit Britain's Atlantic coastline. The southern part of England will be under water. All cities with a boundary with the Atlantic Ocean and the Mediterranean Sea will be flooded. A great flood will come upon many cities of the world. Many ships will be wrecked. Destruction of living creatures in the sea will make it appear bloody.

Chapter Thirteen

Seventh Seal Part 2: Fourth World War and the Greatest Earthquake (2029-2036 A.D.)

Third Trumpet Judgment = Third Bowl of Judgment

Third Trumpet: Judgments on Rivers and Springs	Third Vial (Bowl): Judgments on Rivers and Springs
Then the third angel sounded: And a great star fell from heaven, burning like a torch, and it fell *on a third of the rivers and on the springs of water.* The name of the star is Wormwood. A third of the waters became wormwood, and many men died from the water, because it was made bitter. (Rev. 8:10-11, emphasis mine)	Then the third angel poured out his bowl on the *rivers and springs of water,* and they became blood rivers. (Rev. 16:4, emphasis mine)

The third trumpet of judgment marks the beginning of warfare that will end in the great battle of Armageddon, which is represented by the sixth trumpet of judgment. Therefore, this chapter deals with the most ruthless war in the history of humanity, a war that will start and end in the Middle East. By the end of this horrendous war, one-third of the inhabitants of the earth will have been destroyed.

This is why we need to participate in the rapture so that we will not partake in the wrath of God.

Nuclear Warfare Starts in the Middle East

"A great star fell from heaven" refers to a nuclear bomb that will fall into the Mediterranean Sea. Fish will be poisoned by nuclear chemicals. Many will be destroyed by the heat generated by the bomb. This will be an advanced weapon of mass destruction. Everyone in the world will be terrified by the effect of this great bomb.

Personal Insight: From the Middle East region, including North Africa, *a new Arab leader* will arise whose influence will spread to neighboring countries. This leader will eventually obtain nuclear weapon. This dangerous leader will launch a nuclear missile against Israel in hope of wiping out the state from the surface of the earth so as to finish the task that *the little horn* before him started. Instead, the bomb will hit the Mediterranean Sea and destroy lives in the ocean.

This will be a new Arab leader who replaces the little horn (the Assyrian) who was slain by the appearance of the Lord on the day of rapture. This leader's missile on Israel will hit not only the Mediterranean Sea and poison almost all of the fish in it, but it will also poison the fish in the twelve seas associated with it: the Adriatic Sea, Aegean Sea, Black Sea, Alboran Sea, Ionian Sea, Ligurian Sea, Marmara Sea, Sea of Crete, Sea of Azov, Myrtoan Sea, Thracian Sea, and Tyrrhenian Sea. Many fish will die from the heat generated by the nuclear explosion. Due to this horrendous attack, the Mediterranean Sea will be polluted. Moreover, the regular passage of trade will be disrupted and food prices will go up even more in the region. People living in areas far from the epicenter of the nuclear explosion but supplied by the twelve seas will be tempted to eat fish, even though they know they should not, and many will die both from eating the fish and drinking nuclear-polluted water because they have no access to safe drinkable water.

It is important to note that twenty-one modern states have coastlines on the Mediterranean Sea. They are:

- Europe (from west to east): Spain, France, Monaco, Italy, Malta, Slovenia, Croatia, Bosnia and Herzegovina, Montenegro, Albania, Greece, and Turkey
- Asia (from north to south): Turkey, Cyprus, Syria, Lebanon, Israel, Egypt
- Africa (from east to west): Egypt, Libya, Tunisia, Algeria, and Morocco

A German leader exercising political power over the European Union and the political leader over the alliance of North American countries will move decisively against the new Arab leader for attacking Israel. Moreover, the members of the European Union will feel that they need to stop the war to protect the supply of fuel from the Middle East. For meddling in this Middle East war and for supporting the Jews, the Arab leader in a very bold and unexpected move will declare war against the West. He will use the rest of his arsenal on Europe. This leads to the fourth trumpet judgment.

Fourth Trumpet Judgment = Fourth Bowl Judgment

Fourth Trumpet: Sun Is Affected	Fourth Vial (Bowl): Sun Is Affected
Then the fourth angel sounded: *And a third of the sun was struck,* a third of the moon, and a third of the stars, so that a third of them were darkened. A third of the day did not shine, and likewise the night. (Rev. 8:12, emphasis mine)	Then the fourth angel *poured out his bowl on the sun,* and power was given to him to scorch men with fire. (Rev. 16:8, emphasis mine)

Nuclear Warfare: Europe Attacked

Fourth Trumpet: As a result of the mushroom cloud from the nuclear blast, debris will be sent into the atmosphere. This will cause darkness in the southern part of Europe. Arabs will use weapons of mass destruction against European cities in order to punish Europe for interfering in the Middle East war and for supporting Israel.

Fourth Bowl: Sun-like heat generated by nuclear warfare. (Rev. 16:8-9)

To be scorched with great heat refers to the heat generated by the nuclear confrontation during this time. This will occur between Arab nations and Europe. The explosion will be so awful and the heat so intense that it will seem as if part of the sun was brought to earth. The effect will be felt hundreds of miles away from the epicenter of the nuclear blast. Consequently, the Mediterranean Coast in Europe, particularly in France and Italy, will be almost uninhabitable. The Republic of Malta, Europe's smallest and most densely populated country will be hit. The megalithic temples of Malta, the oldest freestanding buildings on earth, will be destroyed. However, the European Union leader, with the support of North America, will defeat the Arab leader. He will be crushed by the twin leaders of Germany and North America, but this war will further weaken the Western world and allow China to rise to power.

Fifth Trumpet Judgment = Fifth Bowl Judgment = First Woe

The fifth trumpet will introduce us to a great nation whose army is able to cover the earth like a locust. This is the Republic of China. First and foremost, let us examine the rise of China.

The Rise of China: 2022-2029 A.D.

Between 2022 and 2029 A.D., China's military power will be noticed by many. China is currently planning to become the most powerful nation on earth. The assessment of China's military potential was released on October 2, 1998 by Col. Larry M. Wortzel, and his assessment is still valid today. Colonel Wortzel assumed the duties of Director of the United States Strategic Studies Institute in June 1998. From December 1997 to May 1998, he was the director of Asian studies at the U.S. Army War College. As a military intelligence and foreign area officer, he focused his research on China and East Asia. According to him:

> The People's Republic of China (PRC) is seen by many as an economic powerhouse with the world's largest standing military that has the potential to translate economic power into the military sphere. As one of the elements of power, a nation's military potential is based not only on its capability to defeat an adversary, but also its ability to coerce and exercise influence. *China's standing armed force of some 2.8 million active soldiers in uniform is the largest military force in the world.* Approximately 1 million reservists and some 15 million militia back them up. With a population of over 1.2 billion people, China also has a potential manpower base of another *200 million males* fit for military service available at any time. In addition to this wealth of manpower, China is a nuclear power. It has enough megatonnage, missiles, and bombers to hit the United States, Europe, its Asian neighbors, and Russia. For China's leaders, the economy is the most important factor determining future military power. China's military leaders are working to develop the capability to control sea lines of communication, project regional force, and deter the United States and other potential

adversaries in creative ways without matching forces.[15]

Fifth Trumpet: Darkness	Fifth Vial (Bowl): Darkness
Then the fifth angel sounded: And I saw a star fallen from heaven to the earth. To him was given the key to the bottomless pit. And he opened the bottomless pit, and smoke arose out of the pit like the smoke of a great furnace. *So the sun and the air were darkened because of the smoke of the pit.* Then out of the smoke locusts came upon the earth. And to them was given power, as the scorpions of the earth have power. (Rev. 9:1-3, emphasis mine)	Then the fifth angel poured out his bowl on the throne of the beast, *and his kingdom became full of darkness;* and they gnawed their tongues because of the pain. (Rev. 16:10, emphasis mine)

China Is Attacked by Allied Forces: The Fifth Trumpet

Having too few resources available in the world will lead to crisis. Food, energy, housing, and healthcare will be affected severely. People who are suffering will begin to fight those who have surplus. Countries with supplies of gas and energy will be attacked by others in order to take away their oil wells. People will fight over fresh water, fertile lands, and strategic military locations. Highly populated nations like China and India will have to go to war in order to provide food and energy for their own people. Due to the high population density in China, there will be more starving people there than in the rest of the world. Therefore, China

---

[15] http://www.fas.org/nuke/guide/china/doctrine/chinamil. htm (last accessed June 21, 2012)

will become more aggressive to its neighbors, Russia and India.

Personal Insight: War will start as a border clash between China and Russia. There is a railroad on this border which the Chinese will forcefully take over from the Russians. Many military tanks will be used in this great battle, and China will have the upper hand. China will use this opportunity to push further into Russian territory, dividing the country into two and taking over some of Russia's oil fields. The northern territory of Russia will fall into the hands of the Chinese. The invasion of Russia will not stop until the Chinese get to Finland, Norway, Sweden, and Denmark. The loss of lives will be heavy. In order for Russia to survive, she will go into alliance with Europe and North America, and the alliance formed will attack China.

The star falling in Revelation 9:1 refers to a nuclear attack on China by the Allied forces. It is going to strike one of China's most populous cities. A great mushroom cloud will arise from the epicenter of the nuclear blast and cover a whole region of China. The effect will be like that of a great earthquake. One of China's great cities will be destroyed. Millions of lives and billions in property will be destroyed. This attack will be too painful for the Chinese, and peace will no longer be an option. China's military will be loosed upon the world—unrestrained and thirsty for revenge. The People's Liberation Army, which is the unified military organization of land, sea, and air forces of the People's Republic of China, will be highly motivated to attack the Western world. This single event will be the turning point in this war of the East against the West.

China Will Respond with Biological Weapons

> Then out of the smoke *locusts* came upon the earth. And to them was given power, as the scorpions of the earth have power. *They were commanded not to harm the grass of the earth, or any green thing, or any tree, but only those men*

who do not have the seal of God on their foreheads. And they were not given authority to kill them, but to torment them for five months. Their torment was like the torment of a scorpion when it strikes a man. (Rev. 9:3-5, emphasis mine)

China will respond with a multitude of military helicopters against the kingdom of the beast, which is Europe. India will also be in alliance with the West against China. The Chinese army (currently named the People's Liberation Army) invading the kingdom of the beast will be like locusts swarming the land. China will attack Europe and her allies with biological weapons, and it will take about five months to produce a vaccine to neutralize the effect of the biological germs. Many of these biological weapons of mass destruction are being processed now. These weapons will not destroy buildings, only people. Some of the organisms used in this warfare will cause pulmonary complications. Europe, Russia, and India will be severely affected.

Let us examine the symbols given by the Scriptures regarding the destructive locusts that will attack the kingdom of the beast.

The shape of the locusts was *like horses* prepared for battle. On their heads were crowns of *something like* gold, and their *faces were like* the faces of men. They had hair *like* women's hair, and their teeth were *like* lions' teeth. And they had breastplates *like* breastplates of iron, and the sound of their wings was *like* the sound of chariots with many horses running into battle. They had tails *like* scorpions, and there were stings in their tails. Their power was to hurt men five months. And they had as king over them the angel of the bottomless pit, whose name in Hebrew is Abaddon, but in Greek he has the name Apollyon. (Rev. 9:7-10, emphasis mine)

143

John sees metal-coated flying military objects. Hal Lindsey, a well-known prophecy teacher, interpreted the symbols accurately. He wrote:

> John keeps saying, "looked like, something like, resembled, etc." By these qualifying terms, John sought to emphasize that he was aware of describing vehicles and phenomena far beyond his first-century comprehension. So he used symbols drawn from first-century phenomena that "looked like" these marvels of science.
>
> The general outer shape of a helicopter is similar to that of a locust. The phrase "horses prepared for battle" probably means "the attack helicopters" were heavily armored.
>
> The phrase "something like crowns of gold" most likely describes the elaborate helmets worn by helicopter pilots. And "their faces resembled human faces . . ."—as John looked at the front of the helicopter, the face of the pilot appeared through the front windscreen. The appearance of something that looked like a woman's hair could describe the whirling propeller that looked like filmy hair. Remember, John had never seen a large instrument spinning so fast that it couldn't be seen clearly. The term "teeth" probably describes the weaponry projecting from the "chopper"—there is a monster six-barrel cannon suspended from the nose of most attack helicopters today. The "sound of their wings was like many horses and chariots rushing to battle"—those of us who have heard the thunderous sound of many military helicopters flying overhead can relate to this description.[16]

---

[16] Hal Lindsey, *Apocalypse Code* (Parlos Verdes, CA: Western Front Ltd, 1997), 41-43.

Below are pictures of military helicopters.

These machines do, in fact, look very much like the vision the apostle John saw:

(http://en.wikipedia.org/wiki/ File:CSA-2006-02-24-095553.jpg)

(http://en.wikipedia.org/wiki/ File:LCH_TD2_Front.jpg)

According to Michael Rood, a well-known teacher of the Word of God, "The eastern scorpion has a long black tail. The tail that is long and black on a military attack helicopter is the air cooled 7.62 mm cannon that has sting that will put a man down on the ground writhing in agony."[17]

Personal Insight: Warfront will spread from Delhi to Calcutta. Germ warfare will be used by the Chinese against those in Europe, Russia and India and will claim the lives of more than twenty million people. The whole of Asia will fall into the hands of Chinese troops.

This war is called the first woe because of the millions of people who will be destroyed. This terrible war against humanity will be led spiritually by demons and the forces of darkness in heavenly places. According to the Scriptures, "Over them as king they have the angel of the Abyss (of the bottomless pit). In Hebrew his name is Abaddon [destruction], but in Greek he is called Apollyon [destroyer]" (Rev. 9:11, Amplified Bible)

---

[17] Michael Rood, *The Mystery of Iniquity* (Gainesville, FL: Bridge-Logos, 2001), 201.

Sixth Trumpet Judgment = Sixth Bowl Judgment = Second Woe

Sixth Trumpet: From Great River Euphrates to Armageddon	Sixth Vial (Bowl): From Great River Euphrates to Armageddon
Then the sixth angel sounded: And I heard a voice from the four horns of the golden altar which is before God, saying to the sixth angel who had the trumpet, "Release the four angels who are bound at the *great river Euphrates.*" So the four angels, who had been prepared for the hour and day and month and year, were released to kill a third of mankind. Now the number of the army of the horsemen was two hundred million; I heard the number of them. And thus I saw the horses in the vision: those who sat on them had breastplates of fiery red, hyacinth blue, and sulfur yellow; and the heads of the horses were like the heads of lions; and out of their mouths came fire, smoke, and brimstone. By these three plagues a third of mankind was killed—(Rev. 9:13-18, emphasis mine)	Then the sixth angel poured out his bowl on the *great river Euphrates*, and its water was dried up, so that the way of the kings from the east might be prepared. And I saw three unclean spirits like frogs coming out of the mouth of the dragon, out of the mouth of the beast, and out of the mouth of the false prophet. For they are spirits of demons, performing signs, which go out to the kings of the earth and of the whole world, to gather them to the battle of that great day of God Almighty. "Behold, I am coming as a thief. Blessed is he who watches, and keeps his garments, lest he walk naked and they see his shame." And they gathered them together to the place called in Hebrew, Armageddon. (Rev. 16:12-16, emphasis mine)

Chinese Invasion of the Middle East: Armageddon

Sixth Trumpet: A two-hundred-million-man Chinese army will invade the Middle East via the Euphrates River to fight the beast (the German leader) and the false prophet (the leader of the North American countries) at the battle of Armageddon, the worst battle in the history of humanity. One-third of humanity will be destroyed in this devilish massacre. Surely this is the second woe. The invasion of the two-hundred-million-man Chinese army into the Middle East will be like a horde of locusts—very destructive in nature. Oil and natural resources will fuel this horrendous war. Chinese military tanks are described in Revelation 9:17

> And thus I saw the horses in the vision: those who sat on them had breastplates of fiery red, hyacinth blue, and sulfur yellow; and the heads of the horses were like the heads of lions; and out of their mouths came fire, smoke, and brimstone.

What John saw in this vision are military "horses" of the twenty-first century. Michael Rood explained these symbols very well. He writes:

> The horses described here are obviously not of Equine origin . . . *The horses had heads like lions that sat up on their bodies, with a devastating armaments system.* Out of these heads came the ingredients that propel a 155mm howitzer: fire, smoke, and sulfur. Those that sat on top of this battlefield monstrosity were wearing the typical *three-color camouflage* flack jackets and full coverage tanker helmets that are required for all tank personnel. This is another picture perfect description of the battle tanks and the "human wave" forces that are prepared to march into the Mideast from the eastern communist bloc.[18]

---

[18] Michael Rood, *The Mystery of Iniquity* (Gainesville, FL: Bridge-Logos, 2001), 203-204.

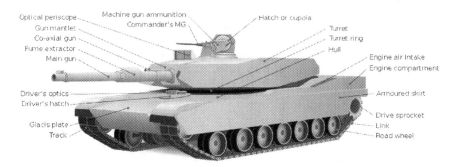

(http://en.wikipedia.org/wiki/File:M1_Abrams-TUSK.svg)

The riders of these battle-ready "horses" have breastplates using a three-color combination: red, blue, and yellow. As discussed above, three-color or four color camouflage is now the standard battle dress in almost all national armies of the world.

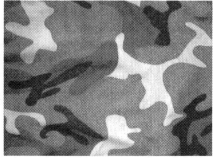

(http://en.wikipedia.org/wiki/
File:Brtish_dpm2.jpg)

(http://en.wikipedia.org/wiki/
File:Pla_camo.jpg)

Examples of four-color desert camouflage

According to Rood: "This is the exact position, clothing, and armament that is found on the battle tanks of every major power on the earth. Those who ride on the tank turret that controls the 155mm 'mouth' that kills as it belches fire and smoke are protected by a required issue camouflage flack jacket. The gunner mans a 50 caliber, air-cooled, belt-fed machine gun with a flash suppresser that looks exactly like a snake with a head. Out of this 'snake' comes a half inch diameter round that 'hurts' very severely."[19]

Sixth Bowl: The shallow end of the Euphrates River will become dry due to severe drought and numerous developmental dam projects established by the governments of Turkey, Iraq, and Syria. There will be a severe drought as a result of the nuclear cloud. It will be one of the most severe droughts in human history. It will be so severe that many rivers, including the Euphrates, will dry up. So severe will be the drought that famine will ensue all over the world. There will be food shortage in many countries. The Middle East and the African continent will be greatly affected.

The following low rainfall countries may have the worst drought in the history of their nations: Burkina Faso, Cape Verde, Chad, Gambia, Guinea-Bissau, Mali, Mauritania, Niger, Senegal and Sudan in Africa, and Afghanistan, Pakistan, Iran, Iraq, Turkey, and Syria in the Middle East. What a great drought! The Euphrates River, the longest and one of the most important and economy-impacting rivers in Southwest Asia, will dry up. What great suffering! What great judgment against humanity! This severe drought will be complicated by the ongoing war between the East and the West.

The Dangerous Influence of Three World Rulers

Three men under the influence of three evil spirits will lead humanity into the war of Armageddon. These three men are leaders from Germany, the United States, and China. This is the war of the East against the West. Europe, the United States, and Russia will be allied against the Chinese and the Arabs. The Western world will be financially attacked by the diversion of oil from their economies to that of China. The West will invade the Middle East via Turkey to take

---

[19] Michael Rood, *The Mystery of Iniquity* (Gainesville, FL: Bridge-Logos, 2001), 204.

over the route for the flow of oil and checkmate the growing power of China in the Middle East. Meanwhile China will invade the Middle East via the Euphrates River in order to protect the treaty signed with the Arab leaders.

> Then I saw three evil spirits that looked like frogs; they came out of the mouth of the dragon, out of the mouth of the beast and out of the mouth of the false prophet. They are spirits of demons performing miraculous signs, and they go out to the kings of the whole world, to gather them for the battle on the great day of God Almighty . . . *And they gathered them together to the place called in Hebrew, Armageddon."* (Rev. 16:13-14, 16, emphasis mine)

The greatest war in the history of humanity—World War IV—will climax on the plain of Megiddo outside the city of Jerusalem. Devastating war will rage on the east of the Jordan River.

The false prophet, who is the political leader of the United States, Canada, and Mexico, will call down fire from heaven to destroy the Chinese army. There is a reference to this in Revelation 13:13: "He performs great signs, so that he even makes fire come down from heaven on the earth in the sight of men." The fire from heaven is a form of advanced weapon used by the beast and the false prophet. It is a laser beam from space directed at the Earth's surface to destroy the Chinese army.

The game plan of the Chinese army will be to overwhelm their enemies by sheer numbers. It is assumed that waves of thousands of soldiers pouring into the Middle East will be too much for even nuclear attack against them to be effective. Gathering their hordes numbering two hundred million, they will move like locusts overland toward the allied armies in the Middle East. They will have already used their military power to overwhelm the Russians. Now they will use the same tactics against Europe and her allies.

They think that enough soldiers will survive the blasts, radiation, and firestorm to defeat the allied armies. Alas, the Chinese will be surprised. An invisible laser beam from space will thwart their plans. Whoever passes through this invisible laser wall will die. Hundreds of millions of Chinese soldiers will pass through unknowingly and die.

Once about two-thirds of the Chinese military have died in the senseless war, their leader will realize that he has made a mistake, but it will be too late to surrender. In an attempt to make for a final push for victory, the Chinese leader will order everyone to be sent into the war. Every able-bodied man, woman, and young adult will be sent. What a disaster! The effect of the laser beam on the invading army is described by the prophet Zechariah:

> And this shall be the plague with which the Lord will strike all the people who fought against Jerusalem: *Their flesh shall dissolve while they stand on their feet, their eyes shall dissolve in their sockets, and their tongues shall dissolve in their mouths.* (Zech. 14:12, emphasis mine)

For over 184 miles, from the plain of Megiddo outside Jerusalem to the great Euphrates River, dead soldiers will litter the ground. This is to fulfill the Word of God:

> And the winepress was trampled outside the city [Jerusalem] and blood came out of the winepress, up to the horses' bridles, for one thousand six hundred furlongs [184 miles]. (Rev. 14:20)

This is the second woe, because in this war, one-third of humanity will be killed. "By these three plagues a third of mankind was killed—by the fire and the smoke and the brimstone which came out of their mouths." (Rev. 9:18)

> "The second woe is past. Behold, the third woe is coming quickly." (Rev. 11:14)

Seventh Trumpet Judgment = Seventh Bowl Judgment = Third Woe

Seventh Trumpet: Thundering, Lightning, Noises, Earthquake, and Great Hail	Seventh Vial (Bowl): Thundering, Lightning, Noises, Earthquake, and Great Hail
Then the seventh angel sounded: *And there were loud voices in heaven,* saying, "The kingdoms of this world have become the kingdoms of our Lord and of his Christ, and he shall reign forever and ever!" . . . Then the temple of God was opened in heaven, and the ark of his covenant was seen in his temple. *And there were lightnings, noises, thunderings, an earthquake, and great hail.* (Rev. 11:15, 19, emphasis mine)	Then the seventh angel poured out his bowl into the air, *and a loud voice came out of the temple of heaven,* from the throne, saying, "It is done!" *And there were noises and thunderings and lightnings; and there was a great earthquake, such a mighty and great earthquake as had not occurred since men were on the earth.* (Rev. 16:17-18, emphasis mine)

Seventh Trumpet: The final manifestation of the wrath of God comes with earthquake, lightnings, noises, thundering, and great hail. This is associated with the worst earthquake in the history of humanity.

Third Woe: This is the third and the final woe.

Jesus Christ and the Saints

After the marriage supper of the Lamb, the saints and the Lord Jesus Christ will descend from heaven. What a glorious sight that will be! The saints make up the armies of heaven.

> I saw heaven standing open and there before me was a white horse, whose rider is called Faithful and True. *With justice he judges and makes war.*

His eyes are like blazing fire, and on his head are many crowns. He has a name written on him that no one knows but he himself. He is dressed in a robe dipped in blood, and his name is the Word of God. *The armies of heaven were following him, riding on white horses and dressed in fine linen, white and clean. Out of his mouth comes a sharp sword with which to strike down the nations.* "He will rule them with an iron scepter." He treads the winepress of the fury of the wrath of God Almighty. On his robe and on his thigh he has this name written: KING OF KINGS AND LORD OF LORDS. (Rev. 19:11-16, emphasis mine)

A Great Bright Star: The Appearance of Christ

The glorious light of the coming of Christ will be seen in heaven. The glory of his appearance with his saints will appear as a very bright star in the sky. For seven days, the star will become brighter and brighter until it becomes like a sun. It will be so bright that the night will appear as day. Its brightness will give the impression that the sun is appearing at night—that there are double suns in the sky. At the climax of this brightness, there will be no darkness for twenty-four hours until the Lord has gained victory over his enemies. This twenty-four-hour daylight will mark the beginning of the millennial reign of Jesus Christ. This phenomenon of double sun is referred to by the Word of God.

And the Lord my God shall come, and all the saints with thee. And it shall come to pass in that day, that the light shall not be clear, nor dark: *But it shall be one day which shall be known to the Lord, not day, nor night: but it shall come to pass, that at evening time it shall be light.* (Zech. 14: 5-7, emphasis mine)

This bright light will cut short the celebration of the European leader (the beast) and the North American leader (the false prophet) who have just conquered the Chinese army and are in the process of setting up a worldwide empire. NASA and other space scientists will come to the conclusion that the trajectory of this bright space object brings it into direct collision with the earth. Therefore, from the United States and Europe, the most powerful nuclear missiles will be launched in a very coordinated manner to knock the object off its collision course. This is to fulfill the Word of God.

> Then I saw the beast and the kings of the earth and their armies gathered together to make war against the rider on the horse and his army. (Rev. 19:19)

The Lord Jesus Christ will speak and his voice will shake the heavens and the earth and there will be great thunder and lightning. The missiles will be destroyed in their flight and the inhabitants of the earth will be terrified. This is to fulfill the Word of God in Revelation 19:15: "Out of his mouth comes a sharp sword with which to strike down the nations."

Mount of Olives: The Mountain of God

The hearts of many inhabitants of the earth will fail them. Having failed to stop the armies of heaven (who are referred to as "aliens") from coming into the Earth's atmosphere, the great armies of the earth will gather together in the mountainous part of Europe for an engagement against the uninvited "aliens." These armies under the leadership of the beast and the false prophet will gather on the Western Alps, which comprise a great mountain system in Europe located in Italy, Switzerland, and France. But the glory and the power of God will come to rest upon the Mount of Olives. That was the same mountain that witnessed the ascension of Jesus Christ into heaven about two thousand years ago.

> And while they looked steadfastly toward heaven as he went up, behold, two men stood by them in

> white apparel, who also said, "Men of Galilee, why
> do you stand gazing up into heaven? This same
> Jesus, who was taken up from you into heaven,
> will so come in like manner as you saw him go into
> heaven." Then they returned to Jerusalem from
> the *mount called Olivet*, which is near Jerusalem,
> a Sabbath day's journey. (Acts 1:10-12, emphasis
> mine)

It shall come to pass that when the glory and the power of
God rests upon the Mount of Olives—when Jesus Christ
has physically descended—that the greatest earthquake
in the history of humanity will occur. *This is the seventh
trumpet.* Jerusalem shall be divided into three, and many
cities of the nations of the world will fall. (Rev. 16:18-19)

The Greatest Earthquake in Human History

> And in that day his feet will stand on the Mount
> of Olives, which faces Jerusalem on the east. And
> the Mount of Olives shall be split in two, from
> east to west, making a very large valley; half of the
> mountain shall move toward the north and half of
> it toward the south. (Zech. 14:4)

Personal Insight: This *global cataclysmic earthquake* will
impact every town, city, nation, and continent of the world.
Every inhabitant of the earth will be affected. *The world
leaders, the beast, and the false prophet and their armies
on the Western Alps and different locations in Europe will be
swept away.* Airplanes, warships, war tanks, and armored
vehicles will be buried. The beast and the false prophet will
be cast alive into lake of fire, because they will be buried
by the great earthquake, fulfilling the Word of God. (Rev.
19:20-21)

Personal Insight: As a result of this great earthquake, the
New Madrid Fault Line that stretches between the Southern
and Midwestern United States will be forcefully pushed
open. The North American continent will be split into two or

more islands. Many great cities, including those in Florida and the Hawaiian Islands, will be no more.

Personal Insight: New York City, Rome, and London will be completely immersed in water. It will be as if those cities never existed. This is to fulfill the Word of God:

> Then a mighty angel took up a stone like a great millstone and threw it into the sea, saying, "Thus with violence the great city Babylon shall be thrown down, and shall not be found anymore." (Rev. 18:21)

Personal Insight: Great earthquakes and super volcanic eruptions within the Atlantic and Pacific oceans will create new mountains and islands that will displace a great amount of water onto many coastal nations. Super volcanic eruptions will cause new mountainous ranges to be formed, especially in the area of the North Sea. This will be associated with new elevations of land above sea level. Also in Antarctica, new elevations above sea level will be found. *For many nations, it will be like the days of Noah.*

Although the flood of this seventh trumpet will destroy many nations, some will escape with little impact. This flood will not be universal like Noah's flood because of the covenant. The destruction of humanity will not be total. Unlike Noah's day when only Noah and his family were saved, several million people will be saved, but millions will perish.

Personal Insight: Huge and mighty waves of great heights will travel across many coastal cities and towns with terrific speed and wipe out many buildings and people in an instant. In addition, many volcanoes will spit out poisonous gas. Living will be very hard for the survivors. This is to fulfill the Word of God:

> I will punish the world for its evil, and the wicked for their iniquity; I will halt the arrogance of the proud, and will lay low the haughtiness of the terrible. I will make a mortal more rare than fine

gold, a man more than the golden wedge of Ophir. *Therefore I will shake the heavens, and the earth will move out of her place, in the wrath of the Lord of hosts and in the day of his fierce anger.* (Isa. 13:11-13, emphasis mine)

Personal Insight: The Island of Japan will be devastated. The Philippines will be no more. Most of Poland will be under water. The African continent will be split into two or more islands. Europe will be split into islands. The coastlines of Russia, China, Europe, the Americas, and India will be under water. This is to fulfill the Word of God:

> Behold, the Lord makes the earth empty and makes it waste, distorts its surface and scatters abroad its inhabitants. (Isa. 24:1)

Personal Insight: Boundaries of many countries as we know them today will no longer exist. New boundaries will be established. The whole world will be thrown into unfathomable chaos. God will change the topography of the earth; there will be rivers in the desert and a highway on the sea. This is to fulfill the Word of God:

> Behold, I will do a new thing, now it shall spring forth; shall you not know it? I will even make a road in the wilderness and rivers in the desert. (Isa. 43:19)

In one day, civilization as we know it will come to an end. Education, medical care, and cities as we know them will come to an end. Capitalism, socialism, and communism will come to an end. Means of transport as we know it will come to an end. Religion as we know it will come to an end. Global financial and banking systems will come to an end; world currency will come to an end; forms of government in the world as we know them will come to a sudden end. The power of sin will be broken. Evil will be overcome. Righteousness will reign for one-thousand years. The saints who descend with Jesus Christ will reign with him for a thousand years. (Rev. 20:1-4)

Chapter Fourteen

The Great Millennium: One-Thousand Years of Peace

There will be a new beginning; God will make all things new. There will be true peace in the world for one-thousand years. Can you imagine that? Ancient enemies in the Middle East will come together in peace and unity. This is to fulfill the Word of God:

> In that day Israel will be one of three with Egypt and Assyria—a blessing in the midst of the land, whom the Lord of hosts shall bless, saying, "Blessed is Egypt my people, and Assyria the work of my hands, and Israel my inheritance." (Isa. 19:24-25)

The saints who came back with Jesus Christ will help the survivors of the wrath of God rebuild the planet. There will be new forms of education and agriculture. There will be new forms of energy and technology. The nation of Israel shall prosper spiritually, temporally, and socially. (Isa. 65:21-25)

A new temple, which will be the fourth temple or the Millennial Temple, will be built in Jerusalem. This temple will be the symbol of the throne of God and his Lamb among the nations. It is described in detail by the prophet Ezekiel in Ezekiel 40-48. Jesus Christ and his saints will help the nation Israel build this temple, fulfilling the Word of God:

> Thus says the Lord of hosts, saying: *"Behold, the
> Man whose name is the BRANCH! From his place
> he shall branch out, and he shall build the temple
> of the Lord;* Yes, he shall build the temple of the
> Lord. He shall bear the glory, and shall sit and rule
> on his throne; so he shall be a priest on his throne,
> and the counsel of peace shall be between them
> both." (Zech. 6:12-13)

When the temple is completed, Jesus Christ will enter this
glorious tabernacle via the outer Eastern Gate, which then
will be shut forever. Although the ruler of Israel may come
into the gate to eat sacrificial meals, he must use only the
entrance room. This is to fulfill the Word of God:

> Then he brought me back to the outer gate of
> the sanctuary which faces toward the east, but
> it was shut. And the Lord said to me, "This gate
> shall be shut; it shall not be opened, and no man
> shall enter by it, because the Lord God of Israel
> has entered by it; therefore it shall be shut." (Eze.
> 44:1-2)

From the entrance of the Millennial Temple, a stream of
water will issue and become a big river that will empty into
the Dead Sea. This river will be referred to as the "river of
water of life" by many because it will bring healing to the
Dead Sea. Moreover, trees that grow on its bank will be
referred to as "trees of life" because their fruits and leaves
will bring healing to the nations. These trees will produce
fruits every month. This is to fulfill the Word of God:

> In the middle of its street, and on either side of the
> river, was the tree of life, which bore twelve fruits,
> each tree yielding its fruit every month. *The leaves
> of the tree were for the healing of the nations.* (Rev.
> 22:2, emphasis mine)

There will be a breakthrough in medical and herbal
sciences that will guarantee long life. Hence, to die at the
age of one-hundred will be to die prematurely. Spiritually,

people will be filled with the knowledge and love of God. Politically, great and small nations will abide in peaceful relationships. The glory of the living God will fill all the earth. This is to fulfill the Word of God:

> No more shall an infant from there live but a few days, nor an old man who has not fulfilled his days; for the child shall die one hundred years old, but the sinner being one hundred years old shall be accursed. (Isa. 65:20)

The Lord Jesus Christ will reign from Jerusalem. He will be a very strong leader, rebuking every form of oppression, creating prosperity and teaching new ways of living. From Jerusalem, guiding principles and laws binding on all nations shall go forth. Those who came with Jesus Christ shall reign with him, fulfilling the Word of God:

> For out of Zion the law shall go forth, and the word of the Lord from Jerusalem. He shall judge between many peoples, and rebuke strong nations afar off; they shall beat their swords into plowshares, and their spears into pruning hooks; nation shall not lift up sword against nation, neither shall they learn war anymore. But everyone shall sit under his vine and under his fig tree, and no one shall make them afraid; for the mouth of the Lord of hosts has spoken. (Micah 4:2b-4)

Chapter Fifteen

Who Is This Christ?

About two thousand years ago, an extraordinary child was born in the Middle East in the land of Israel. His mother was a virgin and his birth was announced by an angel of the Lord. His name is Jesus the Christ. He grew up in the power of God. He did several things that made his followers wonder about him. More importantly, he claimed to be the Son of God, thereby making himself equal with God.

Jesus claimed that he was greater than David (Matt. 22:41-46). Even David, one of the most celebrated leaders of the Jews, had a vision of Jesus Christ in Psalm 110. He saw Christ in his glory and called him Lord. Who is this man who is greater than David?

Jesus made a reference to Abraham, the father of the Jewish nation, as an illustration of his divinity. According to the Scriptures, Jesus' proclamation of his divine identity got him into trouble with a lot of people (John 8:51-59).

Who is this man claiming to be greater than Abraham and all the prophets? Who is this man claiming to be the source of life to those who believe in him? Who is this man claiming to be equal with God?

Jesus claimed to have power to forgive sin, making himself equal with God (Matt. 9:2-8). Who is this Christ with awesome power to forgive sins?

Jesus demonstrated his power over the elements of the universe (Mark 4:37-41). What manner of man is Jesus

Christ that even the wind, the sea, and the elements of the universe obey him?

Jesus claimed to be the subject and the object of the Bible. He claimed that Moses wrote about him and that he is the only one who can guarantee life (John 5:39-47). Who is this man who claimed to know more than Moses and all the religious leaders of his time?

Jesus claimed to be the only source of salvation of humankind. What about Moses and Abraham, the founders of Judaism? What about Muhammad, the founder of Islamic religion? What about Brahmins, the founders of Hinduism? What about Siddharta Gautama, the founder of Buddhism? What about Haile Selassie I of Ethiopia, the most popular Emperor of Ethiopia, the religious symbol of the Rastafari movement? What about the wise King Solomon?

> Jesus said to him, "I am the way, the truth, and the life. No one comes to the Father except through me." (John 14:6)

Who is this man who claims to be the way, the truth, and the life?

Jesus claimed to have the power to raise people from death to life. Publicly, he proclaimed that surely a day is coming when he would raise everyone of those who had trusted him for their salvation from death to eternal life in God's glory. What an audacious claim! Power to bring dead people back to life? Nobody—no prophet in the history of humanity—has made such a claim (John 6:36-40, 51).

Who is this man promising to raise the dead back into joy, peace, and glory of the living God? Who has heard such a claim before? Who is this man claiming to hold the key to death and life?

Jesus made resurrection from the dead one of the pillars of his good news. Jesus claimed that everyone who died believing in him would be raised up on the last day to the glory of God the Father. After the death of Lazarus, a friend of the Lord, Jesus had a discussion with Martha, Lazarus' sister, and he claimed the ability to give, restore, impact, and maintain life.

Now, Lazarus had been dead for about four days when Jesus, the anointed one, came upon the scene. Immediately, Jesus went to the tomb and raised Lazarus up from death, thereby demonstrating his divine ability to guarantee, sustain, and extend life. What a mystery! Who is this man so filled with the Holy Spirit that even death obeys him? This miracle was the last straw for the religious leaders of that time. They would no longer tolerate a man so filled with the awesome presence of the Holy Spirit that many common folks became his followers. The religious leaders conspired against Jesus to have him killed.

Who is this man who single-handedly turned a whole nation downside up? Who is this man who became a nightmare to the religious oppressors of his time? Who is this individual?

Jesus claimed that he would go and prepare a glorious place for everyone who had received him into their hearts. Furthermore, he claimed that he would come back again and take God's people to a place he had prepared for them. Jesus told his faithful disciples about his plan for their lives and future. (John 14: 1-3)

Who is this man who claimed to have the power to go into the heavens and prepare a place for you and I if we dare to believe in him and follow him to the end?

Jesus was crucified like a criminal, died on the cross, and was buried. His disciples were overcome with fear. The power of the Roman government was used to kill this wonderful teacher. But this man refused to stay in the tomb; life refused to succumb to death; light triumphed over darkness. What manner of man is this that even the grave could not hold him?

Jesus Christ, having risen from the dead, appeared to his disciples for a period of forty days. Then something happened at the end of the fortieth day. He ascended. In the sight of his disciples, Jesus suspended the law of gravity and ascended into heaven. What kind of wonder is this? What kind of power is at play here? What kind of being is this man? (Acts 1: 9-11)

The die was cast. Two witnesses from heaven declared that Jesus would physically return to the Mount of Olives where the ascension took place. Can you believe this? This Jesus, who has risen from death, will one day come back to stand on the Mount of Olives. It has now been about two thousand years. Are you really sure that Jesus Christ will come back again?

Who is this man who has influenced the destiny of humanity like none before or after him? This Jesus was an uneducated carpenter, who chose twelve common folks as his disciples, yet his name is revered by scholars around the world. Although he did not write a single book, millions of books have been written about him. Although he was treated as a social outcast by his generation, more than a billion people have come to identify with his name. Although he owned no home, millions of places of worship have been built in his name. He was born in a manger like the least of humanity, yet kings, emperors, celebrities, presidents, and prime ministers, army generals, and Nobel Prize winners have bowed down and worshipped him. Although his public ministry lasted only three-and-one-half years, he is more popular than George Washington, Thomas Jefferson, John Adams, James Madison, Alexander Hamilton, John Hancock, and Benjamin Franklin, who were the Founding Fathers of one of the greatest nations on earth. Although he preached repentance from sin, wickedness, and violence, and although he preached love, humility, and selfless service, he has drawn more followers than Alexander the Great, Julius Caesar, and Napoleon Bonaparte, who were great military geniuses of their generations. Who is this Christ?

Jesus appeared to one of his beloved disciples in the last book of the Bible, also called the Revelation of Saint John. In that revelation, Jesus appeared in his glory and made a full disclosure about his divinity. He said:

> "*I am the Alpha and the Omega, the Beginning and the End,*" says the Lord, "*who is and who was and who is to come, the Almighty*" . . . His head and hair were white like wool, as white as snow, and his eyes like a flame of fire; his feet were like fine brass, as if refined in a furnace, and his voice as the sound of many waters; he had in his right hand seven stars, out of his mouth went a sharp two-edged sword, and his countenance was like the sun shining in its strength . . . "*I am the First and the Last. I am he who lives, and was dead, and behold, I am alive forevermore. Amen. And I have the keys of Hades and of Death.*" (Rev. 1:8, 14-18, emphasis mine)

Now that you have been confronted with the Word of Jesus Christ, you need to make a decision. Either you believe in him or disbelieve; either you reject him or accept him. Either Jesus Christ was making a false claim (thereby making him the greatest fraudster in the history of humanity) or making a true claim (thereby making him the Lord and Savior of humankind). The choice is yours to make. There is no middle ground.

In this book, we have examined the predictions of Jesus Christ; the series of events that Jesus claimed would precede his return. Jesus Christ predicted the course of the end-time generation in the book of Revelation when he opened the seven seals. He predicted a movement for global peace in the first seal and a horse rider that will take away peace from the earth in the second seal. He predicted global economic crisis in the third seal and World War III in the fourth seal. In the fifth seal, he revealed the severe persecution that is coming upon those who keep the commandments of God and hold the testimony of Jesus Christ. He predicted that great tribulation is coming upon the Jews but also proclaimed the resurrection of the saints. In the sixth vial of judgment, Jesus revealed a terrible war that will be fought in the Middle East in a place known as Armageddon. In the seventh vial of judgment, he warned of an earthquake that will be the greatest in the history of humanity. Jesus gave insight into the coming one-world government that will rule the whole earth for three-and-one-half years. While many seers have predicted future events, none can be compared with the authority and finality with which Jesus Christ prophesied about the events that are happening and that will continue to happen within the next two decades. Wisdom demands that we pay attention to the word of this Man from Galilee.

Chapter Sixteen

Conclusion

Jesus is coming back very soon, sooner than many expect. We can see the signs of his coming and hear his footsteps. We can perceive that we are the last generation and that end-time events are unfolding rapidly. On May 14, 1948, Israel became a nation. That day marked the beginning of the end-time generation. Israel is God's fig tree. The prophet Joel, referring to the destruction of Israel, told us so. He wrote, "He has laid waste my vine, and ruined *my fig tree*; he has stripped it bare and thrown it away; its branches are made white" (Joel 1:7). The end-time generation is the one that witnesses the blooming of the fig tree, that is, the restoration of Israel. This generation will not pass away until all last day events, including the rapture, are fulfilled.

Now that we have been counted worthy to bear witness to the end-time events, let us live our lives as the five wise virgins, not the foolish ones.

To be foolish is to become lukewarm in our Christian journey. Many Christians are lukewarm today because his return has been delayed. As a result, the promise of his coming has become dull in their hearing. They have heard it over and over again. Sometime ago, they were ready for his coming; they were very hot for God. But having waited so long, they became distracted. To be foolish is not to carry extra anointing oil for our spiritual journey. To be foolish is to fail to pray and watch for the fulfillment of end-time events. To be foolish is to become skeptical about his coming. To be foolish is to fail to accept Jesus Christ today. Today is the day of salvation; tomorrow may be too late. To be foolish is to miss the rapture, and whosoever misses the rapture will not reign with Jesus Christ for one-thousand years. According to our Lord Jesus Christ, the kingdom is not being prepared for the foolish but for the wise.

To be wise is to live every day of our lives as if it is the last day. To be wise is to know that even if the rapture is delayed, the day I die is the day of *my* rapture. Since my death is not under my control, I worship God, glorify God, and do his will as if today is my last day. To be wise is to make a resolute decision to stand for Jesus Christ to the end—not to be confused, distracted, or frustrated, but to press forward in spite of challenges and crisis, knowing that in spite of problems and difficulties; in spite of persecutions and tribulation; in spite of victories, success, and great testimonies; knowing that nothing, absolutely nothing, can separate us from the love of God. To be wise is to be prepared and ready for him should he come today or seventy years from today. *Always be prepared, for he will surely come.*

It will be like in the days of Noah, before the flood came, people were given the opportunity to repent and enter the Ark. Sadly, only eight people—the family of Noah—received that grace of salvation from destruction. Once again, humanity is confronted with a choice between life and death. Please choose life. Choose Jesus Christ, and you will never regret it. In order to grow spiritually, please find a Bible-believing church and fellowship with other children of God on the same spiritual journey to righteousness, peace, joy, resurrection, and eternal life in Christ Jesus.

Decide for Jesus Christ Now: Are you ready to reign with the Lord Jesus Christ? Are you at peace with God? A void exists in every person's heart that only God can fill. I'm not talking about joining a church or finding religion. I'm talking about finding life and peace and happiness. It is time to escape from the wrath of God. Would you pray this prayer today? Just say, "Lord Jesus Christ, I repent of my sins. I ask You to come into my heart. I make You my Lord and Savior."

Brothers and Sisters, if you prayed that simple prayer sincerely with faith, I believe that you have been "born again." Moreover, you have escaped from God's wrath. The grace of our Lord Jesus Christ, the love of God and the fellowship of the Holy Spirit will be with you for evermore. I encourage you to attend a good, Bible-based church and keep God first in your life.

Remain blessed in Christ Jesus.

Appendix

Calculating the Days from Adam

Whereas the biblical calendar is given in literal years from Adam, the calendar we are using today is designed in B.C. and A.D. To understand many principles related to prophecy, we need to understand how to convert the Bible's calendar to the modern and internationally accepted Gregorian calendar.

The modern calendar puts Jesus Christ in the middle of human history. Events that happened before Jesus Christ are dated B.C. (before Christ) and events that happened after Christ are dated A.D. (*anno domini*, Latin for "the year of our Lord"). This Gregorian calendar ascribes 3975 B.C. as the birthday of Adam.[20] Therefore, in order to convert a given year from Adam to the Gregorian calendar, we can use this formula:

3975 minus "year from Adam" = Gregorian calendar

3975—"year from Adam" = B.C.

For instance, using the genealogies provided to us in Genesis, we know that from Adam to the birth of Abraham is 2008 years. In order to convert this to our modern-day Gregorian calendar, we use the formula 3975-2008 = 1967 B.C. This is why some Bible scholars use 1967 B.C. as the birth year of Abraham.

---

[20]   Frank R. Klassen, *The Chronology of the Bible,* (Nashville, TN: Regal Publishers, 1975), 6.

Secondly, from Adam to the exodus from Egypt is 2513 years. In order to convert this to the Gregorian calendar, we use our formula 3975-2513 = 1462 B.C. This shows that the exodus from Egypt took place in 1462 B.C., which is consistent with the date some Bible scholars have recorded as the date of the Exodus. You can confirm this by Googling "exodus from Egypt 1462 B.C."

Thirdly, from Adam to the completion of the Solomon's Temple is three thousand years. Converting this to Gregorian calendar gives us 3975-3000 = 975 B.C.

Chronology of the Bible from Adam

Can we confirm what these scholars have done? Can we confirm the number of years from the birth of Adam? Our first challenge is to calculate from Adam to the year of the flood using only biblical references.

Name	Age at Son's Birth
Adam (Gen. 5:3)	130
Seth (Gen. 5:6)	105
Enos (Gen. 5:9)	90
Cainan (Gen. 5:12)	70
Mahalaleel (Gen. 5:15)	65
Jared (Gen. 5:18)	162
Enoch (Gen. 5:21)	65
Methuselah (Gen. 5:25)	187
Lamech (Gen. 5:28)	182
Noah at the time of the flood (Gen. 7:6)	600
Total	1656 Note: Converting to modern calendar = (3975-1656) = 2319 B.C.

From Adam to the year of the flood is 1656 years. Therefore, according to the above table, the flood took place in the year 2319 B.C.

Our second challenge is to calculate the number of years from Adam to the birth date of Abraham.

Name	Age at Son's Birth
Adam to the flood	1656
Two years after the flood (Gen. 11:10)	2
Arphaxad (Gen. 11:12)	35
Shelah (Gen. 11:14)	30
Eber (Gen. 11:16)	34
Peleg (Gen. 11:18)	30
Reu (Gen. 11:20)	32
Serug (Gen. 11:22)	30
Nahor (Gen. 11:24)	29
Terah (Gen. 11:32, 12:4)	130 (205-75) Note: Abraham was 75 years old when Terah died at the age of 205 years. Therefore, Terah was 130 years old when Abraham was born.
Total	2008

Birth date of Abraham = (3975-2008) = 1967 B.C.[21]

Our third challenge is to calculate the number of years from Adam to the exodus from Egypt.

---

[21]   Frank R. Klassen, *The Chronology of the Bible* (Nashville, TN: Regal Publishers, 1975), 11.

Events	Years
From Adam to the birth of Abraham	2008
When Abraham was 75 (Gen. 12:4), Abraham was called by God	75
From Abraham's call to the exodus from Egypt (Ex. 12:40-41; Gal. 3:17)	430 Note: According to *Dake's Commentary* on Exodus 12:40: "The whole of the sojourn was from 75th year of Abraham's life when he entered Canaan to the day of exodus from Egypt. The entire sojourning took place in Mesopotamia, Syria, Canaan, Philistia, and Egypt. The sojourning in Egypt was only 215 years, one-half of the 430 of the whole period."[22]
Total	2513

From Adam to the exodus from Egypt is 2513 years. Converting this to our modern calendar = 3975-2513 = 1462B.C.[23]

Our fourth challenge is to calculate the number of years from Adam to the building of Solomon's Temple.

Events	Years
From Adam to the exodus from Egypt	2513
Fourth year of Solomon's reign (1 Kings 6:1; 2 Chron. 3:1-2)	480

---

[22] Finis Jennings Dake, *Dakes Annotated Reference Bible* (Lawrenceville, GA: Dake Bible Sales, 1998), 77.

[23] Frank R. Klassen, *The Chronology of the Bible* (Nashville, TN: Regal Publishers, 1975), 22-23.

The building of the temple lasted for seven years (1 Kings 6:38)	7
Total	3000

This is amazing! 2993 years from Adam, the foundation of the Solomon's Temple was laid:

> And it came to pass in the four hundred and eightieth year after the children of Israel had come out of the land of Egypt, in the fourth year of Solomon's reign over Israel, in the month of Ziv, which is the second month, that he began to build the house of the Lord. (1 Kings 6:1)

The building of the temple lasted for seven years. According to 1 Kings 6:38:

> And in the eleventh year, in the month of Bul, which is the eighth month, the house was finished in all its details and according to all its plans. So he was seven years in building it.

First temple, also known as Solomon's Temple, is completed at 3,000 years from Adam = 2993 years plus 7 years (1 Kings 6:38) = 3000 = 975 B.C.[24]

From Adam to the completion of the first temple (Solomon's Temple) at Jerusalem is three thousand years. What is amazing is that God is counting even when humanity is not paying attention. At the appointed time in history, the temple was completed. What we need to do is convert this three thousand years to our Gregorian calendar using the formula 3975 minus literal years from Adam = Gregorian calendar: 3975-3000 = 975 B.C.

Knowing that three thousand years of human history from the time of Adam ended in 975 B.C., we can easily calculate

---

[24] Frank R. Klassen, *The Chronology of the Bible* (Nashville, TN: Regal Publishers, 1975), 37.

the date for six thousand years from Adam by adding three thousand years to 975 B.C. = 2026 A.D.

Note: By adding three thousand years to 975 B.C., we should get 2025 A.D., but there is no 0 B.C. or 0 A.D., so we jump from 1 B.C. to 1 A.D. Hence, the addition of one year to the result.

Using literal dates from the Scriptures, six thousand years from Adam is going to end in 2026 A.D. Since three thousand years from Adam was related to the building of the first temple in Jerusalem, six thousand years from Adam may be related to a major end-time event, the building of a new temple in Jerusalem. This temple is alluded to throughout the Scriptures (such as in Daniel 9:27, Matthew 24:15, and 2 Thessalonians 2:3-4) and is an event often referred to in end-times literature as the third temple, which we discussed at length in the main text of this book.